P9-BJK-682

BIG ENOUGH TO BE INCONSISTENT

The W. E. B. Du Bois Lectures

BIG ENOUGH

TO BE

INCONSISTENT

Abraham Lincoln
Confronts Slavery and Race

GEORGE M. FREDRICKSON

Harvard University Press

Cambridge, Massachusetts

London, England

2008

Library of Congress Cataloging-in-Publication Data

Fredrickson, George M., 1934–

Big enough to be inconsistent : Abraham Lincoln confronts slavery and
race / George M. Fredrickson.

p. cm.—(W.E.B. Du Bois lectures)

Includes bibliographical references and index.

ISBN-13: 978-0-674-02774-9 (alk. paper)

ISBN-10: 0-674-02774-4 (alk. paper)

1. Lincoln, Abraham, 1809–1865—Political and social views.

2. Lincoln, Abraham, 1809–1865—Relations with African Americans.

3. Slavery—Political aspects—United States—History—19th century.

4. African Americans—Civil rights—History—19th century.

5. State rights—History—19th century.

6. Federal government—United States—History—19th century.

7. Presidents—United States—Biography.   I. Title.

E457.2.F786   2008

973.7092—dc22   2007034018

For Jake and Carlito

Contents

Preface

MORE THAN THIRTY years ago I published an article entitled "A Man but Not a Brother: Abraham Lincoln and Racial Equality."[1] Since then a great deal has been written on this subject, some of it disagreeing with one or more points that I had made, especially my debatable suggestion that Lincoln's racial views remained essentially unchanged until his dying day.[2] In this book I wish to return to the subject and broaden it by incorporating the scholarship of the past three decades as well as devoting greater attention to Lincoln's view of slavery as an institution or state of being, considered apart from the race of its victims.

The book derives from the Du Bois lectures, given at

Harvard University in November 2006. Having always been a great admirer of W. E. B. Du Bois and having been influenced on several occasions by his profound insights into America's racial problems and dilemmas, I accepted this challenge with great eagerness. When I examined what Du Bois had to say specifically about Lincoln, I found inspiration and stimulus for my own investigation of Lincoln's thought and politics. A quotation from Du Bois provided my title and one of my central themes.

I wish to thank Henry Louis Gates and the W. E. B. Du Bois Institute for African and African American Research for inviting me to give the lectures and providing me with the opportunity to reevaluate slavery and race in Lincoln's thought and politics. The strategic aim of this book is to find a middle ground between the hagiographers, who view Lincoln as a consistent and effective opponent of slavery and a sincere, if sometimes politically covert, champion of racial equality, and the debunkers, who are fixated on what they take to be Lincoln's dyed-in-the-wool racism. Needless to say, the former have been much more numerous than the latter, who have appeared, for the most part, during the past forty years. The first chapter of my book describes and analyzes the historiographic polarization that has recently developed between the admirers of Lincoln's egalitarianism and those who see him as just another American white supremacist. The temptation to glorify Lincoln and focus on his virtues is very great. He is commonly thought of as the greatest of our presidents and the embodiment of our national ideals, and it is difficult to deny the power and persuasiveness of this conception. But for all his admirable qualities, Lincoln, like all other presidents, had his limitations. His own ideas and beliefs, especially about African Americans and their place in society, were formed in an intensely racist environment. As a successful politician, he was dependent on the votes of many white Americans who had narrow and bigoted opinions on the issues of the day. In order to be elected he had to be responsive to such attitudes, or at least give them lip service.

None of this should be surprising to good historians. But if this book provides any advance over the reams of previous writing about Lincoln, it is because of its attempt to demonstrate the full complexity and ambiguity of Lincoln's encounter with the great national questions of slavery and race. In some ways, as W. E. B. Du Bois suggested, Lincoln's greatness and the fact that he was sometimes uncertain or confused about what he should do or think are not incompatible: he was "big enough to be inconsistent."

I

❦

A Clash of Images:
Great Egalitarian or Hard-Core Racist?

INTERPRETING THE THOUGHT and actions of
Abraham Lincoln is a difficult enterprise. Ambiguities
and contradictions abound. W. E. B. Du Bois, the
greatest of African American intellectuals, made some
references to Lincoln in the early twentieth century that
provide a good introduction to an assessment of his
ideas and actions relative to slavery and race. As late as
1913, Du Bois seems to have shared the hagiographic
view of the Great Emancipator common to African
Americans in this period. In his pageant *The Star of
Ethiopia*, performed in that year to commemorate the
fiftieth anniversary of emancipation, Du Bois portrayed
Abraham Lincoln as the great man who freed African

Americans or their ancestors from bondage. At one point participants in the pageant chanted: "O brothers mine, today we stand / Where half a century sweeps our ken, / God through Lincoln's ready hand, / Struck off our bonds and made us men."[1] But a few years later in a speech of 1917, Du Bois expressed a more critical view: "The very man who is called the Emancipator declared again and again that his object was the integrity of the Union and not the emancipation of the slaves; that if he could keep the Union from being disrupted, he would not only allow slavery to exist but loyally protect it."[2]

The fullest statement of Du Bois's view of Lincoln came in 1922 in two short articles in *The Crisis*, the NAACP organ he edited. He began the first article with a seemingly demeaning portrait of Lincoln as "a Southern poor white, of illegitimate birth, poorly educated and unusually ugly, awkward, ill-dressed." (The contention of illegitimacy was untrue but widely believed at the time. The rest of the description was reasonably accurate, at least for the young Lincoln.) But Du Bois went on to say that, despite his unprepossessing appearance, Lincoln was "big inside" and had "reserves and depths" that would be revealed in a crisis, when he would prove himself "big enough to be inconsistent—cruel, merciful; peace-loving, a fighter; despising Negroes and letting them fight and vote; protecting slavery and freeing slaves."[3] In a subsequent issue of *The Crisis* Du Bois was forced to respond to the "many readers" who were "hurt by what I said of Lincoln." His response was to concede that Lincoln "was perhaps the greatest figure of the nineteenth century." He was to be admired "not because he was perfect but because he was not and yet he triumphed . . . Out of his contradictions and inconsistencies he fought his way to the pinnacles of the earth and his fight was within as well as without."[4] In the spirit of the Du Bois of 1922, I will attempt in this book to probe the hesitations, inconsistencies, and ambiguities in Lincoln's dealings with slavery and blacks without denying the greatness shown by his ultimate success in ridding the nation of the curse of slavery.

In order to frame the subject more precisely and show the historiographic points of departure for my interpretations, I will look critically at some of the historical literature on the topic of slavery and race in Lincoln's thought and politics and will also say something about the historical context within which Lincoln confronted these issues. In the subsequent chapters I will go back to the original sources, mainly the speeches and writings of Lincoln himself, the more reliable recollections of things he is reported to have said, and the diaries and memoirs of those who were close to him. Further investigation of these sources can provide a more complex and variegated understanding of Lincoln's attitudes and actions than most previous accounts have been able to furnish.[5]

Most of those who have written about Lincoln in the past century or so have tried to draw lessons from his life that would prove relevant to the problems and prospects of their own time. Generally regarded as the greatest and most influential of American presidents, he has attracted the attention of political philosophers, novelists, poets, and champions of various causes, as well as that of professional historians. "Getting right with Lincoln" has preoccupied politicians as well as scholars and writers. Every generation, it seems, invents a new Lincoln, or perhaps more than one.[6] The search for a usable or exemplary Lincoln has normally involved the celebration of his virtues and achievements. But the emphasis has varied. Some have viewed the salvation of the Union as his greatest achievement and hailed him primarily as the architect of the modern American nation-state. Making Lincoln the great unifier and downplaying his role in the abolition of slavery made it possible for white Southerners to share in the adulation of Lincoln that became general by the early years of the twentieth century.[7] Coming later was a shift of emphasis from saving the Union to his role as the "great emancipator" and advocate of black rights, which corresponded with the rise of the civil rights movement in the mid-twentieth century.

Recently, as in the writings of Gary Wills and George P. Fletcher, there has been an effort to combine these interpretations by portraying Lincoln as a great constitutional innovator, the president who took the Constitution of the Founding Fathers, with its emphasis on individual liberty and the decentralization of power, and made it into a document that would enable the federal government to assert itself vigorously on behalf of equality for all Americans. The Gettysburg Address invoked the Declaration of Independence rather than the Constitution as the origin of American nationhood and, according to Wills and Fletcher, made its "proposition that all men are created equal" the keynote of American nationality for the first time. It thus opened the way for the Reconstruction Amendments and subsequent federal efforts to extend equal rights to minorities, women, and the economically disadvantaged.[8]

Although Lincoln has usually been portrayed in a positive or even hagiographic way by those who have written about him, a vociferous minority of critics have viewed him negatively, as a bad example to follow and a malign influence in American history. A school of conservative theorists has decried the very constitutional revolution that some liberal scholars have celebrated, looking back nostalgically on the antebellum republic of limited government and states' rights that Lincoln is alleged to have destroyed. Notable in taking this position are Willmoore Kendall and M. E. Bradford.[9] (Whether Lincoln really intended such a revolutionary redefinition of American nationality and fundamental law is in fact debatable; we shall return to this subject later.)

None of these modern conservative critics have explicitly defended slavery and white supremacy, which is what Lincoln's liberal admirers see him as destroying or undermining. But at an earlier time some unabashed racists claimed Lincoln as one of their own. Thomas Dixon, the novelist and playwright who epitomized the intense racism of the turn of the century, seized upon Lincoln's advocacy of colonizing freed African Americans outside the United States, as well as the apparently white-supremacist statements he made in the 1850s, in order to portray him as a harbinger of

Jim Crow segregation. Lincoln appears in this role in the celebrated film *Birth of a Nation*, based on Dixon's novel and play, *The Clansman*.[10] Reputable modern historians favorable to Lincoln have acknowledged the fact that he sometimes said things that are likely to strike modern sensibilities as blatantly racist. But they have excused such language in the light of Lincoln's opposition to slavery, or they have rationalized it as a necessary concession to an intensely negrophobic Illinois electorate, or viewed it as something Lincoln grew out of during his presidential years. The modern liberal historians who have been most critical of Lincoln have portrayed him as a very hesitant or reluctant emancipator and have sided with the radicals and abolitionists of the time who often condemned him for what they regarded as his conservative reluctance to take strong action against slavery. In these various ways, modern ideological orientations have influenced interpretations of Lincoln. It must be acknowledged, however, that the two most notable recent biographies of Lincoln—David Herbert Donald's, published in 1995, and Richard J. Carwardine's, published in 2003—have both managed to avoid judging him from the standpoint of contemporary liberal or conservative ideologies.[11] But the balance and relative objectivity that characterize these works have been rare in the scholarship about a president who has become a national icon.

Indeed, a remarkable historiographic polarization has recently developed on the subject of slavery and race in Lincoln's thought and politics which can serve as a springboard for my own investigation. I should note at the outset that slavery and racism are not necessarily conjoined; one could be against the bondage of African Americans and still consider them innately inferior and unworthy of full citizenship, or be an apologist for slavery without being a biological racist. (Of course attitudes toward black equality and black servitude often came together and reinforced each other, as in the minds of Southern proslavery ideologues and Northern abolitionists.) Moreover, there was not an automatic one-to-one relationship between thought and politics on these issues. The most difficult problem of interpretation that we shall encounter is distinguishing between Lincoln's genuine convictions and his expedient adaptations to political circumstances or necessities. Sometimes the distinction is exceedingly hard to make, and the historian becomes dependent on intuition and a sense of how a particular utterance or action fits into a larger pattern.

The historiography on these issues that preceded the

modern works with which we will be most concerned has been characterized as Civil War "revisionism," which meant downplaying the slavery issue and attributing the war to other factors, such as political ineptitude. As recently as the 1940s and 1950s, prominent historians such as J. G. Randall and Avery Craven were pooh-poohing the notion that the war resulted from a sectional conflict over the future of slavery. Randall, in his magisterial four-volume study of Lincoln's presidency, made little of his subject's antislavery convictions and treated his racial views in a matter-of-fact way, seeing no reason for either praise or blame. Revisionists also tended to criticize the prewar Lincoln for making slavery a divisive moral issue and thus precipitating a "needless war." In revisionist accounts of the Lincoln-Douglas debates, Douglas was often treated sympathetically as someone who was trying to make his policy of "popular sovereignty" in the territories a device to prevent sectional polarization and the great national cataclysm that could (and did) result. From this perspective, Lincoln's rhetoric and unyielding advocacy of free soil contributed to that polarization and thus made an unnecessary war more likely.[12]

Beginning in the 1960s the historiography of Lincoln and slavery took a dramatic turn, as the subject of his contribution to the black struggle for freedom and equality came to the fore. Martin Luther King and the civil rights movement honored Lincoln for his role in the black freedom struggle, but he fared somewhat less well in the writings of liberal or radical historians. The "neo-abolitionists" of the 1960s and beyond generally found Lincoln to be too conservative and cautious when compared with abolitionists like William Lloyd Garrison and Wendell Phillips, or Radical Republicans like Charles Sumner and Thaddeus Stevens.[13] Not surprisingly, Lincoln's racial views also came under critical scrutiny in an age of ascendant egalitarianism.[14] But a more sympathetic portrayal of Lincoln's emancipation policy emerged in the late 1970s and early 1980s, especially in the writings of Peyton McCrary and LaWanda Cox. Focusing on presidential reconstruction in Louisiana, McCrary and Cox gave Lincoln credit for good intentions and a commitment to the gradual achievement of equal rights for African Americans. What some have taken to be his racial conservatism became, in the words of Cox, necessary adjustments to "the limits of the possible."[15] She meant that Lincoln went as far as circumstances permitted in the direction of racial justice and equality in the course of what McCrary called his "Louisiana experiment." These studies called into question the supposition of previous historians that Lincoln's reconstruction policies, had he survived into the postwar period, would have been similar to those of his successor Andrew Johnson, who sanctioned white supremacy and states' rights against the Radical Republicans who took control of the reconstruction process out of his hands in 1866–1867.

I would now like to jump ahead to some of the most recent works on Lincoln. I want to discuss in some detail four books, two of which follow the McCrary-Cox path and indeed go further than they did in making Lincoln not only a long-standing and fervent proponent of emancipation, but also a principled advocate of equal rights for blacks. In sharp contrast to these admiring, almost hagiographic works are two books that go to the opposite extreme by highlighting Lincoln's racism and reluctance to emancipate. The case for Lincoln as a truly great emancipator and a model for the present is made in Allen C. Guelzo's *Lincoln's Emancipation Proclamation*, published in 2004, and in Richard Striner's *Father Abraham*, published in 2006. The Lincoln who falls far short of modern standards of racial equality and justice is presented most emphatically in *Forced into*

Glory by Lerone Bennett, Jr., published in 2000, and in *What Lincoln Believed* by Michael Lind, published in 2004.

Guelzo argues in his study of the Emancipation Proclamation that Lincoln intended to free the slaves from the moment he took office, and that his apparent hesitation and recalcitrance were pragmatic devices or ploys calculated to create a set of circumstances and a climate of opinion that would make emancipation possible. He characterizes this as a "politics of prudence" which, correctly interpreted, allows us to conclude that "Lincoln's face was set toward the goal of emancipation from the day he first took the presidential oath." "Emancipation for Lincoln," Guelzo maintains, "was never a question of the end but of how to construct the means in such a way that the end was not placed in jeopardy."[16] By making "prudence" Lincoln's great political virtue, Guelzo is in tune with an influential recent tendency in the interpretation of Lincoln's thought and character. In a major work published in 2000, the political philosopher Harry V. Jaffa has contrasted Lincoln's practicality and realism with the ineffectual idealism of the abolitionists and Radicals.[17] Another writer who praises Lincoln for his embodiment of "the 'prudence' and the 'responsibility' of the worthy politician" is William Lee Miller, author of *Lincoln's Virtues*.[18] These works of political philosophy carry some ideological freight. By implication, and sometimes more directly, they are condemning not only the abolitionists who criticized Lincoln for his moderation or conservatism, but also the allegedly self-defeating idealism of some segments of the contemporary left, especially those who make uncompromising demands and seek to fulfill them outside the normal political process, as through mass demonstrations and nonviolent direct action.

Building on this mode of appreciating Lincoln's wisdom and virtue, Guelzo stresses Lincoln's deep hatred of slavery and contends that the question for him was not whether to put slavery on the path to extinction, but how to do it. His preferred method was gradual emancipation accompanied by compensation for slaveowners and the voluntary colonization of the freed blacks outside of the United States. It was only when his efforts to influence the loyal slave states to adopt this policy—and to provide an example for the rebellious states of how they could rejoin the Union relatively painlessly—were unsuccessful that Lincoln was driven to more radical measures. The proclamation of emancipation for the states or parts of states still in rebellion on January 1, 1863, was for Guelzo a great achievement that put African Americans firmly on the path to freedom and equality. "It may be special pleading to claim that Lincoln was in the end the most perfect friend black Americans have ever had," Guelzo acknowledges. "But it would also be the cheapest and most ignorant of skepticism to deny that he was the most significant."[19] The book ends with a lament about Lincoln's declining reputation among African Americans in recent years (a subject to which we will return a bit later).

Richard Striner's *Father Abraham* is in a similar vein, except that it covers Lincoln's entire career and not just the pre-emancipation presidency and is even more laudatory than Guelzo's book. In his coverage of the apparently racist statements that Lincoln made in the 1850s, Striner leans over backwards to put them in the best light possible. He argues that Lincoln was being deliberately ambiguous or equivocal when he made statements that could be interpreted as racist in order to deflect or neutralize Douglas's frequent and fervent appeals to white supremacy and keep the debate focused on the morality of slavery. In other words, Lincoln did not really mean what he said or was thought to have said. (In the minds of those who defend Lincoln for his "prudence," duplicity in a good cause can be a virtue.) Striner asks whether Lincoln's professed horror at the prospect of intermarriage was "a statement of principle"—or were such comments merely "expedient concessions"?[20] Although he does not answer the question directly, Striner clearly leans toward the second possibility. As a closet racial egalitarian who was publicly committed only to putting slavery "in course of ultimate extinction," the Lincoln of *Father Abraham* comes across as a Machiavellian manipulator in pursuit of a worthy end. The greatest problem he faced, according to Striner, was the intense racism of most white people in antebellum Illinois and in the North as a whole during the war. Lincoln's efforts as president to initiate "a gradual phaseout of slavery" required him to proceed in such a way as to avoid or minimize a racist backlash against the prospect of emancipation.[21]

At times, in other words, Lincoln was forced to pander to a white supremacist electorate as he maneuvered toward the abolition of slavery. Like some other historians, Striner views Lincoln's advocacy of colonization during the war as a device to assuage racist fears of emancipation rather than a reflection of his sincere belief that (as he told a delegation of blacks in August 1862) both races would be better off if they were totally separated. "Lincoln's motive for colonization," Striner writes, ". . . was his fear that racial prejudice would undermine the cause of liberation unless, somehow, the racial issue could be gradually defused."[22]

The case against the image of Lincoln as an egalitarian "friend of the Negro" is made most insistently in Lerone Bennett's *Forced into Glory*, a book that is the culmination of a gradual process of African American disenchantment with Lincoln. Until well into the twentieth century, Lincoln was adulated as "the great emancipator" by most blacks. Pictures of Lincoln adorned the walls of many African American homes, and the day of emancipation (whenever it was thought to have occurred) was celebrated as a holiday. Booker T. Washington described Lincoln in 1891 as "that great man, 'the first American.'"[23] On the fiftieth anniversary of the Emancipation Proclamation, blacks in several cities held mass celebrations. It was Du Bois, in the 1922 articles in *The Crisis* quoted earlier, who became the first major black leader of the twentieth century to question Lincoln's credentials as a thoroughgoing and consistent champion of racial justice and equality.

Despite the aura of adulation surrounding the Lincoln image, pioneer black historians of the first half of the twentieth century wrote surprisingly little that was directly about him, preferring to record the achievements of African Americans themselves. It was not until 1962 that a black historian undertook a book-length study of Lincoln and his relationship to blacks. Benjamin Quarles's *Lincoln and the Negro* is a careful, well-documented account that calls attention to Lincoln's personal relationships with blacks, as well as the actions he took that affected them. For example, William de Fleurville ("Billy the Barber") not only cut Lincoln's hair but also was represented by him in real estate transactions. Quarles provides much evidence of the deep affection that most blacks developed for "Father Abraham," as he became the instrument of their freedom. He concludes with an eloquent affirmation: "Negroes of the Civil War years and after could find strength for the struggle by reflecting upon the life of a man who . . . had said that this nation could not endure half slave and half free; a man who . . . had called upon his generation to highly resolve that America should have a new birth of freedom; and a man who . . . had exhorted his countrymen to finish the great work they were in."[24]

Quarles's book was published in the midst of the civil rights era, just a year before Martin Luther King gave his "I have a dream" speech in front of the Lincoln

Memorial. Respect for Lincoln and his legacy among African Americans reflected the mood of optimism about the achievement of racial equality and fraternity that prevailed in the early 1960s, culminating in the Civil Rights Acts of 1964 and 1965. But soon the mood began to change. A forerunner of this shift was Malcolm X. Already in the early 1960s, according to the historian Eric Foner, he was urging blacks "to 'take down the picture' of Lincoln—that is to place their trust in their own efforts to secure racial justice rather than waiting for a new white emancipator."[25] The urban riots, a growing recognition of the persistence of black disadvantage, and the rise of the Black Power movement encouraged a general reassessment of Lincoln among black intellectuals. Julius Lester, in his classic statement of Black Power ideology, *Look Out Whitey! Black Power's Gon' Get Your Mama*, published in 1968, found it to be "not only misleading, but a lie, to depict Lincoln as the Great Emancipator."[26] The fullest manifestation of this revisionism was the article "Was Abe Lincoln a White Supremacist?" which Lerone Bennett, previously the author of two major works on African American history, published in *Ebony* in February 1968.[27] His answer to the question was an emphatic "yes." Black veneration for Lincoln as a friend of African

Americans and a champion of their rights had been a huge mistake, he concluded.

For the next thirty years Bennett continued his investigation of Lincoln and race, and the result is a very long book that is meant to be the definitive treatment of the subject. *Forced into Glory: Abraham Lincoln's White Dream*, published in 2000, is an angry and bitter assessment of what Bennett considered a great misunderstanding of Lincoln's character and motivations. The book gathers all or most of the racist or racially insensitive comments that Lincoln made that are in the historical record and takes them at face value, as statements of principle rather than of political expediency. Bennett presents a strong case for the contention that Lincoln shared some of the prejudiced beliefs about blacks that were prevalent among white Americans in the mid-nineteenth century. Some other historians have used the same evidence to reach a similar conclusion, at least about the pre-presidential years.

What is most original and provocative about Bennett's account is his contention that Lincoln was not really opposed to slavery as an institution but rather defended and protected it until circumstances forced him to act against it. "Based on his record and the words of his own mouth," Bennett concludes, "we can say that the 'great emancipator' was one of the major supporters of slavery in the United States for at least fifty-four of his fifty-six years."[28] Congress, he contends, attempted to free the slaves of disloyal masters through the Confiscation Act of 1862 but was stymied because of Lincoln's failure to enforce it. The Emancipation Proclamation was therefore a backward step, designed by Lincoln to preserve as much of slavery as possible. The preliminary proclamation of September 1862 in effect suspended the operation of the Confiscation Act, and the final one freed fewer slaves than were already entitled to liberty under the congressional legislation. Emancipating only those in areas still in a state of rebellion did not immediately free a single slave, whereas vigorously enforcing the Confiscation Act could have freed all except those whose masters had remained loyal to the Union. Lincoln's hesitant, vacillating, and limited emancipation policy was driven, Bennett contends, by the exigencies and circumstances of the war and by political pressure from the Radicals; it did not represent antislavery conviction. If Lincoln could have saved the Union without abolishing slavery, he would have happily done so. The title of the book expresses Bennett's thesis concisely: Lincoln was "forced into glory." One factor forcing his hand, which Bennett acknowledges but might have emphasized more than he does, was the mass desertion of blacks from Southern plantations. By crossing into Union lines, they made themselves available for service to the Northern cause. Some historians have argued that slaves did more to free themselves by voting against slavery with their feet than Lincoln did by proclaiming emancipation.[29]

The book's subtitle suggests a second main theme— Lincoln's dream of an all-white America. Bennett pays great attention to Lincoln's long-standing and persistent advocacy of the colonization of freed blacks outside of the United States. Despite verbal assurances that colonization would be voluntary, it would, Bennett believes, have inevitably involved coercion and would have amounted to a form of "ethnic cleansing." Sometimes Lincoln used the term "deportation" instead of "colonization." It was one thing to encourage individuals to emigrate voluntarily; it was quite another to promote and facilitate the departure of an entire racial or ethnic group. As for the assertion of Lincoln apologists that promoting colonization was a ploy to make emancipation more palatable to white supremacist Americans by alleviating their fears of the social consequences of freeing millions of blacks, Bennett counters what he calls this "fork-tongued argument" by contending that the propaganda for colonization exacerbated racial prejudice rather than mitigating it.[30]

Although most white historians who have reviewed or taken notice of *Forced into Glory* have criticized it rather severely as a tendentious and polemical work, they have found few factual errors in it and have acknowledged the validity of parts of the argument. Even James McPherson, in his generally unfavorable review in the *New York Times*, conceded that "this book must be taken seriously. Bennett gets some things right. Lincoln did share the racial prejudices of his time and place. He did support the idea of colonizing blacks abroad."[31] Clearly the most debatable aspect of Bennett's thesis is not that Lincoln was a white supremacist (at least up to 1863), but rather that he never really opposed slavery in principle or tried to work against it.[32]

The book is clearly driven by ideology—Bennett's deeply held belief that the situation of blacks in the United States was not fundamentally changed by emancipation or even by the civil rights movement and continues to be separate and unequal. Lincoln shares the blame for this failure because his actions fostered the illusion that racial justice and equality had been achieved or were readily achievable. In his effort to wean blacks from the false belief that Lincoln was their benefactor and convince them that they must fight for rights on their own rather than looking to seemingly well-disposed whites for inspiration and leadership, Bennett might appear to be embracing a black nationalist or separatist orientation. But such an interpretation would not be strictly accurate. Bennett includes among the "Real Emancipators" on the book's dedication page not only Frederick Douglass, Harriet Tubman, Nat Turner, and Sojourner Truth, but also John Brown, Wendell Phillips, Charles Sumner, and Thaddeus Stevens. By praising whites who were more radical than Lincoln on the emancipation issue and who indicated that they considered blacks their equals, Bennett is valorizing an antiracist radicalism rather than a separatist black nationalism. Bennett concludes the book by again invoking the antislavery whites who criticized Lincoln's conservatism during his lifetime, along with the black heroes of the struggle, and makes an appeal to true believers in equality "to choose between slavery and freedom." He argues that "a choice for or against Lincoln today is a choice for or against a certain kind of politics. It is a choice for or against masters, slaves, fugitive slave laws, moderation, and militants. Above all else it is a choice for or against slavery, the slavery that defined

George Washington and Abraham Lincoln and the slavery that is still walking the streets of America."[33] How might this choice against Lincoln express itself? The only concrete programmatic recommendation in *Forced into Glory* is some form of reparations for the descendants of slaves.

Although most white historians and critics have written off this book as being too stridently polemical to be considered reliable history, Bennett has one notable white defender—Michael Lind, the well-known essayist and political commentator. Lind's *What Lincoln Believed*, published in 2004, finds Bennett's interpretation persuasive: "Although Bennett's book was widely criticized for its prosecutorial tone, his scholarship was irrefutable. With familiar documents as well as obscure sources, Bennett documented a Lincoln whose attitudes were no less racist for being widely shared among the white Americans of his time." Lind agrees with Bennett that "in his career in Illinois and in national politics, Lincoln not only supported racial segregation but sought to ban black migration to Illinois." Lind then criticizes the "many white historians" who prior to Bennett's book "refused to confront the fact of Lincoln's racism candidly. Instead they downplayed his opposition to black social and political equality and to the migration of free as well as enslaved blacks to the North and West."[34] If the books by Guelzo and Striner are any indication, Bennett's message did not get through to most white historians, Lind being a conspicuous exception. Guelzo discusses Bennett briefly and very critically in his lament about the shift in black opinion of Lincoln from admiration to disdain, while Striner does not mention him at all, although he does list Bennett's book in his bibliography.[35]

But Lind's *What Lincoln Believed* differs significantly in tone and overall purpose from Bennett's book. Lind disapproves of Lincoln's racism but is not especially angered by it; he clearly does not view it as fatally detracting from the greatness of his achievement as a politician, statesman, and exemplar of American democratic values. Despite his highly favorable assessment of Lincoln in general, Lind devotes more attention to Lincoln's racial attitudes than any other historian except Bennett, concluding that throughout his career Lincoln was "not only a nationalist but also a white-racial nationalist who thought that the American national community should be limited to Anglo-Americans and European immigrants."[36] He interprets Lincoln's prewar opposition to the spread of slavery to the territories as the product of a desire to keep the territories lily-white by excluding all blacks, whether slave or free. More than that, Lincoln allegedly aspired to make the population of the entire country exclusively white—a goal to be achieved by colonizing all blacks, slave or free, somewhere outside the United States. More thoroughly even than Bennett, Lind documents Lincoln's commitment to the colonization enterprise and contends, contrary to the view of most historians, that it is "not clear that by his death Lincoln had abandoned his belief in colonization." He gives some credence to a recollection of General Benjamin F. Butler, which most historians now consider spurious, that Lincoln asked him in 1865 to make a logistical study that would answer the question of "whether the Negroes can be exported" *en masse.*[37]

One might think that such a thorough and categorical description of Lincoln's racism would lead to a negative evaluation of his career, but in this case it does not. Lind is not defending or endorsing Lincoln's racism. He finds "the moral low point of Lincoln's career" in a previously unnoticed suggestion in his December 1862 message to Congress that Northern states fearful of an influx of blacks as a result of emancipation could pass laws to exclude them, as Illinois and some other states had done before the war.[38] What Lind does admire about Lincoln is his effort to defend democratic republicanism (albeit a racially circumscribed version of it) at a time when it was in retreat throughout the world because of a resurgence of reactionary authoritarianism, especially in Europe. As a conservative, small "d" democrat, Lind also wishes to save Lincoln from the clutches of modern-day liberals by placing him firmly in the tradition of capitalistic economic nationalism established by Alexander Hamilton and Henry Clay. Hence, despite his dyed-in-the-wool racism, Lincoln remains for Lind the foremost advocate of America as a model of democracy for the rest of the world.

The Bennett-Lind view of Lincoln as a die-hard racist has manifested itself in somewhat milder form in another recent book, Barry Schwartz's *Abraham Lincoln and the Forge of National Memory*. As a sociologist with an interest in symbols rather than in the historical circumstances that created them, Schwartz does not examine Lincoln's ideas and actions in any detail, but he makes his viewpoint clear when he asserts that "Abraham Lincoln was no civil rights champion." He favored "the colonization (deportation) of all former slaves and free blacks. No aspect of Lincoln's life, however, was more distorted during the peak of the civil rights movement than his position on race relations." Schwartz raises a searching question for those historians, like

Guelzo and Striner, who celebrate Lincoln's fundamental egalitarianism: "Many present-day admirers assume that his friendly statements on racial justice [made late in the war], reflect his true sentiments, while his earlier race-baiting arose from political necessity. Many others . . . assume that Lincoln's call for separation and colonization reflected his true feelings, while his public recognition of black rights and interests was induced by irresistible pressures from within his own party."[39]

I would add that there is also a third possibility: Lincoln's attitude toward blacks and his beliefs about race may have changed significantly during the war years. He may have evolved from being a racial separationist into someone who viewed African Americans as potentially equal citizens of a color-blind democracy. This is a possibility that must be explored along with both conceptions of an unchanging Lincoln—the white supremacist and the closet egalitarian simply awaiting his chance to become the great emancipator. I would like to examine the evidence for and against these alternatives in an effort to develop a more complex and nuanced appreciation of slavery and race in Lincoln's thought and politics than is provided by either the Guelzo-Striner or the Bennett-Lind representations.

But before doing this, it may be useful to prepare the

ground by asking what baseline or standard should be used for judging Lincoln's thought and actions. Neo-abolitionist historians profess to derive their standard from the abolitionists of Lincoln's own time. The radical antislavery egalitarianism of the 1850s and 1860s demonstrates what was possible in that historical context, and these historians take Lincoln to task for falling short of a standard set by Garrison, Phillips, Sumner, and Stevens. Critics of this orientation contend that such a judgment really derives from present-day liberal attitudes toward race and is therefore ahistorical. They contrast the practicality and prudence that allowed Lincoln to carry out emancipation with the unrealistic, ineffectual idealism and romanticism of the antislavery zealots. The political philosopher Harry V. Jaffa, in his recent book entitled *A New Birth of Freedom*, evaluates Lincoln from a philosophical perspective derived from Aristotle and Leo Strauss and portrays his "politics of prudence" as the expression of a timeless rationality based on a belief in natural law.[40] Jaffa may have a point about the character of Lincoln's own belief system, but to present it as having an eternal or transhistorical validity goes against the practice of most historians, who assume that the past is over and done with and that one studies it to appreciate the mutability and variability of human experience, not to illustrate or exemplify transcendent philosophical truths.

An alternative way of evaluating Lincoln would be to place him firmly in his own time and place, viewing his opinions on slavery and race in relation to the broader climate of opinion on these matters. A value judgment is still possible. If we accept as an article of faith the contemporary belief in human freedom and equality and acknowledge that there has been some ethical progress in human history—as represented most dramatically perhaps by the abolition of slavery and the discrediting of racism and gender inequality—we can explore the extent to which Lincoln reflected or departed from the political and social morality of his contemporaries, and whether he was in the vanguard of progress or trailed behind it. A summary of the broad currents of thought and action concerning slavery and race in the period leading up to the Civil War will provide the context for a fuller exploration of Lincoln's intellectual and political development.

By the time of Lincoln's birth in 1809, the sectional division between slave and free states had already taken place. The American Revolution had been fought on the principle that "all men are created equal; that they are endowed by their Creator with certain inalienable rights; that among these are life, liberty, and the pursuit of happiness." As Lincoln later noted, it was generally understood at the time of the nation's founding that, in theory at least, "all men" included African Americans. Immediately after the Revolution, slavery came under attack as contrary to the principles on which American independence was based. Beginning with Massachusetts and Pennsylvania, a process of gradual emancipation began in the Northern states. Even in Virginia, the state with the largest number of slaves, the institution seemed to be losing its hold in the 1780s and 1790s, as a rash of voluntary manumissions was accompanied by some serious proposals for gradual emancipation. In the Deep South, however, especially in South Carolina and Georgia, the institution had taken deep root, and these states would probably not have consented to join the Union created by the Constitution if the federal government had been granted the power to interfere with slavery within the states. But there is evidence that many of the Founding Fathers hoped for its eventual elimination or, in Lincoln's later words, "ultimate extinction."[41]

Precedents for restricting the spread or expansion of slavery, in the hope that it might wither away and die, were the Northwest Ordinance of 1787, which prohibited the importation of slaves into the area north of the Ohio that would become the states of Ohio, Indiana, Illinois, Michigan, and Wisconsin, and the banning of the African slave trade in 1808. But by the time the prohibition of the slave trade went into effect, just prior to Lincoln's birth, the tide had turned in Virginia in favor of the perpetuation of slavery, partly as a result of racial prejudices and anxieties. Slavery may have been regarded by many as an evil, but it was a necessary one if it was assumed that large numbers of free blacks and whites could not possibly coexist in the same society. Simultaneous with this hardening attitude toward blacks was the stronger economic foundation for the institution of slavery in the lower South resulting from the invention of the cotton gin and the spread of short-staple cotton cultivation.[42]

The first political crisis involving slavery occurred when Lincoln was eleven. The Missouri Compromise of 1820, which would become a touchstone for Lincoln, admitted Missouri to the Union as a slave state, but prohibited slavery in the rest of the Louisiana Purchase on a line drawn west from Missouri's southern border. The furor that preceded the compromise demonstrated that strong feelings against slavery were developing in the North and in favor of it in the South. But the resolution of the crisis established a precedent for compromise between the sections on issues involving the expansion of slavery.

The next crisis arose during the Mexican War, when Representative David Wilmot of Pennsylvania proposed in 1846 that slavery be banned in all the territories that might be acquired from Mexico as a result of the war. Lincoln, who was now serving in Congress, voted several times in favor of the Wilmot Proviso. After the treaty of Guadalupe Hidalgo and the acquisition of New Mexico and California, the question arose as to the status of slavery in these new territories, and the sectional conflict heated up again. Advocates of "Free Soil" formed a third party that competed in the presidential election of 1848. But the Whig candidate Zachary Taylor was elected (with Lincoln's support). Taylor's plan to admit New Mexico and California to the Union as free states, thus bypassing the territorial stage during which the status of slavery would have to be determined, was unacceptable to the South and its Northern allies in the Democratic Party. After Taylor died in office, a new sectional compromise was hammered out in Congress. Its principal features were the admission of California as a free state; the organization of New Mexico into a territory in which slavery could be established if the inhabitants desired it; the abolition of the slave trade in the nation's capital; and the passage of a draconian new fugitive slave law, giving slaveowners a much better chance of capturing runaways who had made it across the Mason-Dixon line.[43]

The sectional modus vivendi achieved by the Compromise of 1850 lasted only four years. The Kansas-Nebraska Act of 1854, which was proposed by Lincoln's arch-rival from Illinois, Stephen A. Douglas, opened the way for the possible expansion of slavery into territories from which it had been prohibited by the Missouri Compromise. Douglas's formula of "popular sovereignty," which allowed actual settlers at some point to vote slavery up or down, was anathema to the Free Soil movement, which by 1856 had coalesced into a new and more inclusive political party committed to keeping slavery out of the territories, namely the Republicans. The majority of the new party's support came from former northern Whigs like Abraham Lincoln, although there was a substantial minority of ex-Democrats. The Kansas-Nebraska Act led to a miniature civil war between proslavery and free-state settlers in Kansas. The Republicans cited "Bleeding Kansas" and the effort to make it into a slave state as evidence of a "slave power conspiracy." Belief in such a conspiracy seemed to be confirmed in 1857 when the Supreme Court in the Dred Scott decision denied the right of the federal government to prohibit slavery in the territories and declared the Missouri Compromise to be unconstitutional. Further proof of what Republicans saw as the aggressive advance of slavery came in 1857–58, when President Buchanan attempted to force the admission of Kansas as a state despite overwhelming evidence that the majority of Kansans wanted to keep slavery out. At this point Lincoln enters the picture as a major participant, debating with Douglas in the Senate race of 1858, and being elected to the presidency in 1860.[44]

This thumbnail sketch of the national political context from which Lincoln's antislavery politics derived does not tell us much about the environmental crucible from which his specifically racial attitudes may have emerged. In order to assess the extent to which he reflected or transcended the popular racism of the time, we have to look closely at race relations in Lincoln's home state of Illinois, which may have been the most negrophobic of all the Northern states. Except to the extent that it involved Lincoln personally, historians have for the most part neglected the political and social conditions in antebellum Illinois, including its race relations. General accounts of the circumstances of black life in the free states, such as Leon Litwack's classic *North of Slavery* and Eugene Berwanger's *The Frontier Against Slavery*, have of course touched on Illinois, but Charles Zucker's unpublished dissertation of 1972, "The Free Negro Question: Race Relations in Antebellum Illinois," remains the only full account of the intense racism that prevailed in the state.[45] Much of what follows concerning the white supremacist climate of opinion that Lincoln encountered every day (and could hardly avoid being influenced by) is based on Zucker's scholarship.

The majority of settlers in antebellum Illinois, especially in the southern and central parts of the state, came, like Lincoln, from the slave states on the other side of the Ohio River: Kentucky, Tennessee, Virginia, and North Carolina. Most had been non-slaveholding farmers who had no love of the peculiar institution and the way it engrossed the best land and created a privileged planter class. If these settlers were hostile to slavery as an institution, they were also hostile to blacks and wanted to have as little to do with them as possible. One thing that was wrong with slavery in their minds was that it required living in proximity to blacks. But not all the early settlers were antislavery. Some in fact brought slaves with them and attempted to keep them, if not as chattel property, at least as lifetime indentured servants. In 1824 there was a serious effort in Illinois to fully legalize slavery through a constitutional convention. When the referendum authorizing the convention was defeated, Illinois was denied the opportunity to develop a slave-based economy. Nevertheless, residual pockets of slaveholding remained in corners of the state throughout most of the antebellum period.[46]

A principal consideration in the generally successful effort to exclude slavery was the desire to keep Illinois all white, or as white as possible. Opposition to proposals for the legalization and extension of quasi-slavery—the long-term indentured servitude reserved for blacks only—was driven by revulsion at the prospect that these blacks would someday become free. In Illinois as in Indiana and other states of the Old Northwest, various "black laws" were passed that discouraged free blacks from entering the state and discriminated against those who were already there, denying them, for example, the right to vote, serve on juries, or even testify in court. As early as 1813, before Illinois became a state, the territorial legislature prohibited the immigration of free blacks. In 1829, the regulations impeding free black entry were strengthened when the state legislature passed a comprehensive "black code" that discriminated against blacks in every aspect of public life.[47] The dominant attitude was expressed succinctly in 1828 by an Illinois state senator. Having blacks in the state "even as servants," he opined, ". . . is productive of moral and political evil . . . The natural difference between them and ourselves forbids the idea that they should ever be permitted to participate with us in the political affairs of our government."[48] A new constitution was placed before the electorate in 1848, which contained a Negro exclusion clause that was voted on separately; it was approved by more than 70 percent of those who cast ballots. Lincoln's Sangamon County was a relative hotbed of anti-black sentiment, counting 1,483 votes for exclusion and only 148 against.[49]

In 1853, Illinois enacted what the historian Eugene Berwanger has called "undoubtedly the most severe anti-Negro measure passed by a free state." It stipulated heavy fines and even prison sentences for anyone (other than slaveowners just passing through with their slaves) who brought blacks into the state—possibly to act as servants or low-paid workers. Blacks who independently crossed the border into Illinois and remained for more than ten days were subject to a fine of 50 dollars (a substantial sum at the time), which had to be paid immediately. If, as would normally be the case, the accused could not pay the fine, his labor would be auctioned off to the highest bidder for a term negotiated at the time of the sale. After completing his service, the illegal immigrant was required to leave the state in ten days. If he failed to do so, his fine and presumably his length of service would be doubled. Some Illinois newspapers condemned this particularly harsh and draconian law, but most of them still supported some method for excluding African Americans from the state, as earlier legislation had attempted to do. Lincoln, who was out of politics at the time, took no public stand on the law. The minority of whites who had principled objections to the legislation and to black exclusion in general were concentrated in northern Illinois, where many of the settlers had come from the Northeast (a few of them were even abolitionists). As a result of an abject failure to enforce the law in this part of the state, the black population of Illinois actually grew during the 1850s from 5,436 to 7,628. Most of the black newcomers gravitated to Chicago and the surrounding area, where they could hope to find jobs and avoid being exposed to the intense racism that prevailed in the southern and central parts of the state.[50]

What implications for Lincoln's views on slavery and

race might be derived from the political and social con-
texts in which he operated? As an ambitious politician,
Lincoln had to be acutely aware of public sentiment.
He could hardly stake out positions that were contrary
to what was generally believed by the electorate at a
time when he was running for office or otherwise par-
ticipating in political campaigns. But there were some
issues on which the public was sharply divided, such
as the question of the future of slavery in the federal territories. The great Lincoln historian Don E.
Fehrenbacher has argued that Lincoln's "prelude to
greatness" came when he pushed the morality of slavery
to the forefront of debate in the senatorial contest
with Douglas in 1858. Thus he helped keep the Republican Party committed to containing slavery and putting it "in course of ultimate extinction."[51] But a more
cynical interpretation, also based on the facts that
Fehrenbacher uncovered, is possible. Douglas's opposition to the Lecompton Constitution for Kansas, for
which President Buchanan sought congressional approval despite the opposition of the vast majority of
the territory's inhabitants, made him a de facto opponent of the expansion of slavery. Since Lincoln's electoral chances in 1858 depended on his ability to head off
Douglas's co-optation of the territorial issue, it was

good politics for him to raise abstract moral considerations and associate Douglas's "popular sovereignty" policy with the defense of slavery and its right to expand. Differing evaluations of the "House Divided" speech and of the Great Debates show how difficult it is to distinguish political calculation from moral principle in Lincoln's statements and actions in respect to slavery.

How the intensely hostile attitude toward free blacks affected Lincoln's stand on racial issues during his Illinois years is also difficult to determine. It is clear that no one who did not at least pay lip service to white supremacy could get elected to a statewide office in Illinois. Did Lincoln mean the things he said about blacks and race relations in the Great Debates, or was he simply dissembling in order to get himself elected? Neither alternative puts him in a very favorable light. One way to overcome the sharp dichotomy between the closet egalitarian and the hard-core racist would be to acknowledge that "racism" is an imprecise umbrella term and that there is a plurality of orientations that might be considered racist or racialist, some of which may be more benign or less malignant than others. This hypothesis will be explored in the next chapter.

2

Free Soil, Free Labor,
and Free *White* Men:
The Illinois Years

LINCOLN DID NOT concern himself much about slavery before the Kansas-Nebraska Act of 1854 made the status of slavery in the territories a major political issue. As he explained in a speech in 1858: "Although I have always been opposed to slavery, so far I rested in the hope and belief that it was in course of ultimate extinction. For that reason it had been a minor question with me."[1]

There is no reason to doubt that he had disapproved of slavery from an early age. The first public statement of that disapproval came when Lincoln was serving his first term in the Illinois state legislature in 1837: he voted against a resolution condemning the abolitionists and their doctrines and affirming the right under the Constitution to own slaves where permitted by state law. It is not entirely clear why Lincoln voted against this resolution; for the next twenty-five years he would maintain that the Constitution protected slavery in the states and that abolitionists did more harm than good. The record of the debate does not clearly reveal the reason for his vote. According to the historian Douglas Wilson, Lincoln's opposition may have arisen after he offered an amendment affirming the right of Congress to abolish slavery in the District of Columbia and had seen it go down to defeat.[2] What the record does clearly reveal is that a month later, Lincoln and a colleague who had also voted against the resolution issued a formal statement of protest, which could not be debated because it came at the very end of the session. Intended perhaps to counter the impression that the original resolution had given a moral sanction to slavery, the statement affirmed as a principle "that the institution of slavery is founded on both injustice and bad policy." But Lincoln and his collaborator then went on to agree with the original resolution in saying that "the promulgation of abolition doctrines tends rather to increase than abate its evils," and that "the Congress of the United States has no power to interfere with the institution of slavery in the different states." Next, however, came what may have been the nub of the disagreement: "The Congress of the United States has the power under the Constitution to abolish slavery in the District of Columbia; but that power ought not to be exercised except at the request of the people of said district."[3]

This statement anticipated Lincoln's public position on issues involving slavery in the 1840s and 1850s. As a congressman in 1849, Lincoln drafted a law meant to abolish slavery in the District of Columbia with the consent of its free inhabitants. Although he voted several times for the Wilmot Proviso excluding slavery from the territories acquired in the Mexican American War, the District of Columbia proposal, which went nowhere, was apparently the only time he took the initiative on an issue concerning slavery during his term in the House of Representatives.[4] After 1854, the question of slavery in the territories came to the fore, and Lincoln took a strong stand against the expansion of black bondage to places where it had been prohibited under the Missouri Compromise. What the 1837 protest foreshadowed was Lincoln's rejection of slavery as unjust and immoral, combined with a very limited or constrained sense of what could be done about it within the American legal and constitutional structure. Because the Constitution contained a fugitive slave clause, Lincoln included in his District of Columbia proposal of 1849 a provision that empowered District authorities to arrest and return to their owners all fugitives from the neighboring slave states; moreover, despite private reservations, he did not openly oppose the draconian Fugitive Slave Act of 1850.

Before probing further the conservative constitutionalism that severely constrained Lincoln's ability to take political action based on his moral objections to slavery, it might be useful to seek an explanation for the antislavery sentiments that were already there by 1837. Some aspects of Lincoln's childhood, for example, were likely to have predisposed him against slavery. In his 1860 campaign autobiography, Lincoln recalled that his family moved from Kentucky to Indiana "partly on account of slavery; but chiefly on account of the difficulty of land titles in Ky."[5] Many settlers crossed the Ohio to escape the limitations that slavery seemed to place on the opportunities of non-slaveholding farmers to acquire land and status, and the Lincolns may have shared this attitude. Some historians have speculated that religious influences also nurtured Lincoln's antislavery predilections when he was a child in Kentucky. The ministers of the Calvinistic Baptist church to which the Lincoln family belonged reputedly disapproved of slaveholding, but only as a personal sin and not as an object of political or social concern. These "hard-shell" Baptists had a predestinarian resistance to missions and reform movements of all kinds, which would have included agitation against slavery.[6] To some extent, Lincoln may have derived his fatalism, his sense that there was an inscrutable Providence at work over which human beings had little or no control, from this early religious influence. This mind-set could translate into the belief that while slavery was an evil, sinful institution, it would come to an end only when God willed it. A theme of Lincoln's eloquent Second Inaugural Address was that God had imposed the Civil War as a judgment on the nation for tolerating slavery and was now willing its abolition.

A more personal and influential source of Lincoln's early bias against slavery was his resistance to farm labor, which he considered a form of servitude. Not only did Lincoln work without recompense on the family farm, but as a teenager he was rented out to work on other people's farms and forced to turn all his earnings over to his father. In the words of the historian Michael Burlingame, "As a youth Lincoln was like a slave to his father."[7] What Lincoln would find most evil in slavery was not its physical cruelty and sexual exploitation of women (as was the case for Harriet Beecher Stowe), but rather its denial to workers of the fruits of their labor and the right to rise in a competitive free-labor society in which, as Lincoln would put it in 1861, all would have "an unfettered start, and a fair chance, in the race of life."[8] One of Lincoln's fullest statements of this basic ideology is found in a speech he gave in New Haven, Connecticut, in 1860: "When one starts poor, as most do in the race of life, free society is such that he knows he can better his condition." After offering himself as an example of such a poor man who got ahead, he went on to sum up his social ideal: "I want every man to have a chance—and I believe a black man is entitled to it—in which he *can* better his condition—when he may look forward and hope to be a hired laborer this year and the next, work for himself afterward, and finally to hire other men to work for him!"[9] Obviously, slavery is anathema to such a social and economic vision. As an advocate and exemplar of a color-blind, free-labor ideology, there was no way that Lincoln could justify the enslavement of fellow human beings.

But these antislavery sentiments did not make Lincoln an abolitionist—far from it. The belief that abolitionism only made matters worse, as set forth in the 1837 statement, did not change during Lincoln's Illinois years. His attitude was set forth succinctly in a letter of 1845. It was a "paramount duty of us in the free states, due to the Union of the states . . . to let slavery of the other state alone." But it was "equally clear, that we should never knowingly lend ourselves directly or indirectly, to prevent slavery from dying a natural death."[10] Lincoln's hope for the ultimate demise of slavery, while sincere, was more utopian dream than political program. In his 1842 speech before the Washington Temperance Society of Springfield, he concluded by looking forward to the "Reign of Reason . . . when there shall be neither a slave nor a drunkard on the earth."[11] What Lincoln recommended in that address as an antidote to drunkenness was gentle persuasion rather than denunciation or coercion. For the other evil, slavery, he seemed to offer little more.

Given the fact that slavery contradicted some of his deepest beliefs, what prevented Lincoln from becoming an antislavery radical, like some of his fellow Republicans in 1856 who had earlier supported the radical Liberty Party in 1840 and 1844 and the Free Soil Party of 1848? One factor was undoubtedly political ambition. As his law partner William Herndon put it, "his ambition was a little engine that knew no rest."[12] An out-spoken and radical antislavery position would have doomed Lincoln's chances for elective office in central Illinois. But to maintain that Lincoln was simply acting out of expediency would do him an injustice. He may have been constrained by the exigencies of an Illinois political career, but he had sufficient integrity to find principled and intellectually defensible justifications for the stands that he took.

Unlike the abolitionists, who either repudiated the Constitution entirely (as did Garrison) or strained to find an interpretation that would permit direct action against slavery in the states, Lincoln both revered the Constitution and believed that it provided no basis for abolition. He could have proposed an amendment banning slavery, but in 1856 he made it clear that the Constitution should be left alone: "Don't interfere with anything in the Constitution. That must be maintained, for it is the only safeguard of our liberties."[13] The Constitution that Lincoln upheld allowed for action against slavery in areas under federal jurisdiction, but not where state law sanctioned it.

Behind Lincoln's constitutionalism was a more generalized reverence for the law. This legalism came out most clearly in Lincoln's first memorable public address—his speech on "The Perpetuation of Our Political Institutions," presented to the Young Men's Lyceum of Springfield in 1838. The context was a number of recent incidents of mob violence, one being the lynching of a mulatto in St. Louis; another (referred to more obliquely) was the killing of the abolitionist editor Elijah Lovejoy in Alton, Illinois. Lincoln saw such incidents as evidence of "an increasing disregard for law which pervades the country; the growing disposition to substitute the wild and furious passions, in lieu of the sober judgments of courts, and the worse than savage mobs for the executive ministers of justice."[14] To counter vigilantism, lynching, and civil disobedience of any kind, Lincoln urged "a strict observance of all the laws," which did not mean, however, that "there are no bad laws." The proper response to bad laws was to work for their repeal through legally constituted means, "but while they continue in force, for the sake of example, they should be religiously.observed."[15] This was obviously a far cry from the "higher law" doctrine of the abolitionists. Putting the matter in the strongest possible terms, Lincoln called upon his listeners to let "reverence for the laws . . . become the *political religion* of the nation."[16]

One of the factors that lay behind the intense reverence for the law that Lincoln expressed in the Lyceum Address was his sense that there was a competition for the mind of the nation between two professions—lawyers and clergymen. Lawyers stood for reason, moderation, and the resolution of disputes through calm deliberation and judicious compromise. Clergymen and their avid followers, in contrast, stood for emotionalism, perfectionism, and an uncompromising commitment to absolute truths and ideal solutions to complex problems. (This distaste for religious zeal may help to explain why Lincoln never joined a church or supported movements with a clerical leadership. In his speech to the Washington Temperance Society in 1842, for example, he clearly distanced himself from the revivalist, evangelical approach to the reform of manners and morals.) Above all, it was the lawyers and their reverence for the law that could protect the nation from the disruptive passions arising from the slavery issue, passions that might end up threatening the Union itself.[17]

Lincoln's constitutionalism and legalism as impediments to antislavery activism were therefore part and parcel of his reverence for the Union, which of course had its legal basis in the Constitution. In 1854, in his first major speech against the Kansas-Nebraska Act, Lincoln made the following admission: "Much as I hate slavery, I would consent to the extension of it rather than see the Union dissolved, just as I would consent to any GREAT evil, to avoid a GREATER one."[18] What becomes clear is that action against slavery had a lower priority in Lincoln's pre-presidential political thought than reverence for law, maintenance of order, obedience to the Constitution, and the preservation of the Union. If it is legitimate to call the abolitionists "radicals," it is equally justifiable to describe Lincoln as a "conservative" of a certain kind—conservative in his respect for con- stituted authority and his resistance to reformist mili- tancy.

Another difference between Lincoln and the anti- slavery radicals—both those who disdained the politi- cal process and those who tried to work within it— concerned the subject of race. The relevant question was not so much whether whites and blacks were in- nately equal or unequal, but whether or not they could live together in the same society as legal and political equals. Not all antislavery radicals were convinced of the innate equality of the races, but they all considered blacks to be potential fellow citizens who would suc- ceed or fail on their individual merits if accorded equal rights and opportunities. Furthermore, not all of those who denied the possibility of civil equality believed that blacks were inherently inferior. Some of the founders and supporters of the American Colonization Society believed that the problem was ineradicable white prejudice and not black incapacity. Once settled in Liberia, these colonizationists believed, blacks would erect a worthy civilization.[19]

Lincoln was clearly one of those who could not readily envision a society in which blacks and whites could live in harmony as legal and political equals. He did not heap abuse on blacks or take the lead in the enactment of discriminatory "black laws," and his few personal relations with blacks, as with "Billy the Barber," seem to have been cordial. But he made no objection to the laws, not even to the blatantly oppressive exclusion law of 1853. When in 1858 the black abolitionist H. Ford Douglass entreated him to sign a petition calling on the state to accord to blacks the most minimal of civil rights—the right to testify in court—Lincoln summarily refused.[20] In his early career he was not above exploiting race for partisan purposes. In a speech supporting the Whig presidential candidate William Henry Harrison against the Democrat Martin Van Buren in the election of 1840, Lincoln took the latter to task for voting at the New York constitutional convention of 1821 in favor of allowing some free Negroes the right to vote.[21] He also joined with some fellow Whigs to edit a campaign paper that accused Van Buren of the heinous crime of allowing the testimony of free blacks against a white naval officer. "Should not Mr. Van Buren be called the 'NEGRO WITNESS CAN-DIDATE'?" the paper asked.[22]

The principal inspiration for Lincoln's conception of race relations and the ultimate destiny of African Americans was Henry Clay, whom Lincoln described in 1858 as "my beau ideal of a statesman, the man for whom I fought in all my humble life."[23] In 1864, Lincoln is reported to have told an ex-Whig congressman that they shared a reverence for Clay: "and I tell you I never had an opinion upon the subject of slavery in my life that I did not get from him."[24] In 1852 Lincoln gave a full account of the ideas he derived from Clay in an eloquent eulogy for the recently deceased statesman from Kentucky. Clay, Lincoln affirmed, "ever was on principle and feeling opposed to slavery" and advocated gradual emancipation in Kentucky. Although Clay believed in the basic humanity of blacks, he owned slaves himself. Lincoln's explanation for this apparent anomaly was that Clay was born into a society in which slavery was deeply entrenched and did not see "how it could at *once* be eradicated without producing a greater evil even to the cause of human liberty." Consequently Clay rejected both extreme views on slavery—the defense of it as a "positive good" and the call for its immediate abolition. In endorsing Clay's antipathy to the abolitionists, Lincoln added some invective of his own: "Those who would shiver into fragments the Union of these States, tear to tatters its now venerated constitution; and even burn the last copy of the Bible, rather than slavery should continue a single hour, together with all their more halting sympathizers, have received and are receiving their just execration." Lincoln also condemned "those who for the sake of perpetuating slavery are beginning to assail and to ridicule the white-man's charter of freedom—the declaration that all men are created equal."[25]

The curious phrase "white-man's charter of freedom" has been taken by one historian to mean that Lincoln did not consistently adhere to a belief that the Declaration of Independence included blacks as men entitled to the rights to life, liberty, and the pursuit of happiness.[26] But over and over again Lincoln insisted that blacks were indeed among the men "created equal" under the terms of the Declaration. What in all likelihood he meant to convey with this phrase was both a historically accurate understanding of who actually acquired their freedom as an immediate result of the American Revolution, and a warning that a denial of the Declaration's assertion of human rights could prepare the way for the enslavement of whites as well as blacks.

Henry Clay's solution for the problem of slavery and race was gradual, compensated emancipation accompanied by the colonization or deportation of the freed blacks. (For many years, as Lincoln pointed out, Clay had served as president of the American Colonization Society.) Lincoln endorsed the program of the Colonization Society and saw the expatriation of free or freed blacks as facilitating emancipation. The abolitionists had repudiated colonization, viewing it as a concession to racial prejudice, a denial of the possibility of Christian brotherhood, and a means of perpetuating slavery by removing the troublesome free blacks who set a bad example for those in bondage.[27] But Lincoln would have none of that. With eloquence and conviction, he made the eulogy to Clay a vehicle for his own affirmation of colonization: "If as the friends of colonization hope, the present and coming generations of our countrymen shall by any means, succeed in freeing our land from the dangerous presence of slavery and at the same time, in restoring a captive people to their long-lost fatherland, with bright prospects for the future; and this so gradually that neither races nor individuals shall have suffered by the change, it will indeed be a glorious consummation."[28]

Notable in this statement is the assertion that blacks had "bright prospects" in Africa. In Lincoln's formulation and the one that he attributed to Clay, colonization was not so much a kind of "ethnic cleansing" or the expulsion of an undesirable population as an Exodus-like return of a captive people to its Promised Land. (It might be noted that some of Lincoln's black nationalist contemporaries, such as Martin Delany and Henry Highland Garnett, argued at times for black repatriation to Africa in somewhat similar terms.) Although Lincoln was advocating a separation of the races, he did so in this instance without suggesting that the races were inherently unequal in capacities. Blacks, he implied, have capabilities, perhaps as great as those of whites, but they could realize them only in Africa or at least outside the United States. It would remain true that in his public pronouncements Lincoln avoided speaking contemptuously of blacks or consigning them to a subhuman status, although he did on occasion tell crude "darky" jokes, and he enjoyed minstrel shows despite their demeaning racial stereotypes.

The first full and comprehensive statement of Lincoln's views on slavery and race came in the Peoria speech of 1854. Most of the points that Lincoln made for the rest of the decade can be found in this address. The personal context was Lincoln's reentry into politics after a hiatus of five years. After his one term in Congress and his failure to get the patronage appointment he thought he deserved for the support he gave to Zachary Taylor in 1848, he returned to the practice of law on a virtually full-time basis. He recorded no immediate reactions to the Compromise of 1850, but like the Whig Party as a whole he later indicated his acquiescence, despite the blatantly unjust fugitive slave law that was one of its provisions. It was the passage of the Kansas-Nebraska Act in 1854 that was the occasion for Lincoln's return to politics. In this case, ambition and honest conviction seemed to coincide perfectly. Since the act repealed the Missouri Compromise and thus made it possible for slavery to take root in Kansas and Nebraska by means of "popular sovereignty," it ended the tradition of quid pro quo sectional compromise that had been the stock-in-trade of Lincoln's model statesman, Henry Clay. In Lincoln's view slavery now had a kind of national sanction that it had never possessed before.[29] During the debates with Douglas in 1858, Lincoln explained his return to active politics four years previously. "I have always hated slavery," he said, ". . . but I have always been quiet about it until this new era of the Nebraska bill began. I always believed that everybody was against it, and that it was in course of ultimate extinction."[30] When he announced his public opposition to the Kansas-Nebraska Act, Lincoln did so as a Whig who hoped to mobilize his party against the expansion of slavery. More radical opponents of the Act were thinking rather of a new party which would unite the "conscience Whigs" of the North with the minority of Democrats who were also in favor of prohibiting the expansion of slavery. An anti-Nebraska coalition won control of the state legislature in 1854 and Lincoln almost got elected to the United States Senate, but his candidacy foundered on the refusal of the free soil Democrats to vote for someone who still considered himself a Whig.

In the Peoria speech, Lincoln described the "declared indifference" to the spread of slavery professed by Stephen A. Douglas and other supporters of the Kansas-Nebraska Act as "covert real zeal" for it. In one of his strongest statements of antislavery conviction, Lincoln expressed his abhorrence of the policy: "I hate it because of the monstrous injustice of slavery itself. I hate it because it deprives our republican example of its just

influence in the world—enables the enemies of free institution, with plausibility to taunt us as hypocrites."[31]
But despite his hatred of slavery, Lincoln admitted that
he had no plan of action that promised to bring about
its timely eradication. Southerners could not be blamed
for keeping blacks in servitude. "If all earthly power
were given to me," Lincoln confessed, "I should not
know what to do as to the existing institution. My first
impulse would be to free all the slaves and send them
to Liberia—to their own native land." But, however
promising colonization might be as a long-term solution to the problem, "its sudden execution is impossi-
ble." Another option was freeing blacks and keeping
them in America as "underlings," but that might not
"better their condition." A third alternative was freeing
them and making them "politically and socially" the
equal of whites (as the abolitionists were proposing).
"My own feelings will not admit of this," Lincoln confessed, "and if mine would the great mass of white people will not. Whether this feeling accords with justice
and sound judgment, is not the sole question, if indeed,
it is any part of it. A universal feeling whether well or
ill-founded can not be safely disregarded."[32] A constant
element in Lincoln's political thought was a deferential
and somewhat fatalistic respect for deep-seated popular

attitudes. In the Temperance Speech, referring to the difficulty of eliminating alcohol consumption at a time when most people saw no harm in it, he averred that "the universal *sense* of mankind is an argument or at least an *influence* not easily overcome."[33]

In his statement on the ubiquity and rootedness of white supremacist feelings, Lincoln declared that such prejudices were inevitable in a biracial society and admitted that he shared them. But he was unable to make the claim that racial bias and discrimination conformed to any principles of justice or morality—indeed, he suggested the contrary. Prohibition of slavery in the territories constituted a moral stand against slavery, but not one that was calculated to benefit blacks. (Except perhaps, some free-soilers imagined, in the very long run when the slave population confined to the Southern states swelled to the point that gradual emancipation followed by colonization had to be taken seriously as a solution to overpopulation and the threat of massive slave rebellions.) Elsewhere in the Peoria speech, Lincoln appealed directly to white prejudice when he asserted that "the best use" to be made of the territories was to provide "homes for free white people." This could not be the case if slavery was allowed there: "Slave States are places for poor white people to remove

FROM; not to remove to. New free states are the places to go to better their condition."[34] Here Lincoln's views correlated closely with his own personal experience as a poor migrant from the slaveholding South to the free state of Illinois, where he had greatly bettered his condition. But his own Southern origins and associations (his wife, Mary Todd Lincoln, was from a slaveholding Kentucky family) made him sympathetic to what he viewed as the tragic predicament in which white Southerners found themselves.

Some historians have justified Lincoln's position on slavery and race in the 1850s as a prudential or pragmatic manifestation of antislavery politics that accomplished as much as was possible under the circumstances.[35] Recognizing the limitations created by the Constitution and public opinion, he was, it has been argued, challenging slavery in the only realm where he considered it vulnerable to attack—its status in the federal territories. But the Peoria speech manifested a real tension—indeed a contradiction—between Lincoln's veneration of the Declaration of Independence as the expression of enduring truth and his concessions to white supremacy. After noting the obvious conflict between slavery and the principles of the Declaration, he offered a succinct summary of what those principles added up to: "Allow ALL the governed an equal voice in government and that, and that only is self-government." But then he went on to invoke "the argument of NECESSITY, arising from the fact that blacks are already among us," to explain why his interpretation of the Declaration did not require "political and social equality between blacks and whites."[36] If we take him at his word, he was confessing that the United States could not claim to have achieved self-government, since even free blacks did not have "an equal voice in government." Deep-seated white racism clearly trumped the egalitarian principles of the Declaration and thus contradicted the nation's creed. Although Lincoln found slavery to be immoral and hoped for its demise, he made no comparable moral argument against political and social exclusion on grounds of race.

Lincoln developed and extended the basic contentions of the Peoria speech when he ran for the Senate against Stephen A. Douglas, who was up for reelection in 1858. After becoming a Republican and a leader of the party in Illinois, Lincoln watched with great concern the increasing power of the slaveholding interest in national affairs. Especially troubling was the Supreme Court's Dred Scott decision of 1857, which declared the Missouri Compromise unconstitutional and affirmed the right of slaveholders to take their property into all the federal territories. It also ruled that all blacks, free or slave, were ineligible for American citizenship. In his speech on the decision, Lincoln described it as a repudiation of the Declaration of Independence because it sanctioned slavery and thus denied the humanity of blacks. Anticipating that Douglas would try to discredit the Republicans by interpreting their recognition of the right of blacks to "life, liberty, and the pursuit of happiness" as a commitment to their social and political equality with whites, even to the extent of intermarriage or "amalgamation," Lincoln prepared his defenses. He acknowledged "a natural disgust in the minds of nearly all white people to the idea of an indiscriminate amalgamation of white and black races." But he protested "against the counterfeit logic that concludes that, because I do not want a black woman for a slave I must necessarily want her for a wife. I need not have her for either, I can just leave her alone. In some respects she is certainly not my equal; but in her natural right to eat the bread she earns with her own hands without asking leave of anyone, she is my equal and the equal of all others."[37]

This minimalist, "free labor" interpretation of the natural rights set forth in the Declaration of Independence can be contrasted with the abolitionists' conviction that political and social equality was necessary to protect life, liberty, and the pursuit of happiness; and also, at the other extreme, with Douglas's ultra-racist denial that the Declaration meant to include blacks when it referred to "all men." In a formulation that he would repeat in the Great Debates, Lincoln contended that the Declaration "intended to include all men, but they did not intend to declare all men equal in all respects . . . did not mean to say all were equal in color, size, intellect, or moral capacity." Furthermore, the authors of the Declaration did not mean to suggest that equality could be immediately or quickly attained: "They meant simply to declare the right so that the enforcement of it might follow as fast as circumstance should permit."[38] However, given Lincoln's professed hostility to interracial marriages, it is difficult to envision any circumstances under which inequality of "color" would be overcome. Color-blind equality would presumably include the right to marry outside one's racial group, something that Lincoln clearly found unacceptable. At another point in the Dred Scott speech, Lincoln attempted to turn the miscegenation issue against Douglas. After noting that they were "a thousand times agreed" on the horrors of miscegenation,

Lincoln noted that most mulattoes "have sprung from black slaves and white masters." Keeping slavery out of the territories would serve to prevent amalgamation: "If white and black people never get together in Kansas, they will never mix blood in Kansas."[39]

Lincoln's bid for the Senate seat held by Douglas began officially on June 16, 1858, when he addressed the Republican convention that had just endorsed his candidacy. The "House Divided" speech was the most radical, or at least the most radical-sounding, public statement that Lincoln had yet made. In a letter of 1855, Lincoln had asked the question: "Can we as a nation continue together *permanently—forever*—half slave and half free?" But he was not yet ready to provide an answer. "The problem," he confessed, "is too mighty for me. May God, in his mercy, superintend the solution."[40] By late 1857 he had come to the definite conclusion, as he revealed in a draft speech, that "the government cannot endure permanently half-slave and half free." And here for the first time he invoked the biblical quotation that he would employ in the speech to the Republican convention: "A house divided against itself cannot stand."[41] In the final formulation in the "House Divided" speech itself, Lincoln predicted that the house would ultimately cease to be divided: "Either the opponents of slavery, will arrest the further spread of it, and place it where the public mind shall rest in the belief that it is in course of ultimate extinction; or its advocates will push it forward until it becomes lawful in all the states."[42]

The speech provoked the charge from the Democrats that Lincoln's rhetoric encouraged sectional conflict and threatened the survival of the Union. Lincoln's close friend Leonard Swett recalled after the war that it had seemed to him at the time that "nothing could have been more unfortunate, or inappropriate" from a practical political standpoint than this seemingly militant pronouncement.[43] It was often cited, along with William H. Seward's assertion that there was an "irrepressible conflict" between slavery and freedom, as evidence of the Republicans' quasi-abolitionism and the threat to sectional peace and harmony that it represented. But a close reading of the speech reveals that it was not as radical as it seemed at first glance or was represented as being. Essentially, Lincoln was warning against the expansion and nationalization of slavery rather than proposing or anticipating its abolition. "Ultimate extinction" was something one might hope for in the distant and almost unforeseeable future, not a plan of action that went beyond keeping slavery out of the territories.

As Lincoln would hypothesize in a speech of 1859, slavery "may long exist, and perhaps the best way for it to come to an end peaceably is for it to exist for a length of time."[44] In a letter to the editor of the *New York Times*, written when he was president-elect in 1860, Lincoln denied that he was "pledged to the ultimate extinction of slavery."[45] As we have already seen, Lincoln's conservative constitutionalism made individual state action the only possible means of eradicating slavery where it already existed. (Even a constitutional amendment, the means by which slavery was ultimately abolished, was out of the question. Lincoln was opposed to meddling with the Constitution, but even if he had not been, there was no possibility in 1858 of an amendment being approved by a two-thirds vote of Congress and ratified by three-quarters of the states.)

The "House Divided" speech was relatively conservative in another sense. After setting forth as alternatives the containment of slavery, which would encourage the belief that it was "in course of ultimate extinction," or the legalization of slavery "in all the States, old as well new—North as well as South," Lincoln posed the question: "Have we no tendency to the latter condition?"[46] The rest of the speech is devoted primarily to alleging that there was a conspiracy to nationalize slavery, beginning with the Kansas-Nebraska Act and culminating in the Dred Scott decision, a conspiracy in which Douglas was allegedly implicated. The speech can therefore be regarded as a defense of the status quo before 1854 against those conspiring to overthrow it by making slavery legal everywhere. In a later speech in 1859, Lincoln would contend that the "chief and real purpose of the Republican party is eminently conservative. It proposes nothing save and except to restore the government to its original tone in regard to this element of slavery, and there to maintain it, looking for no further change in reference to it than that which the original framers of the government themselves expected and looked forward to."[47]

If the 1858 speech was not as radical as it could be made to appear by taking some of its phrases out of context, the question remains as to why Lincoln would take the political risk of sounding as extreme as he did and opening himself to the charge that he was an abolitionist. The answer, as Don E. Fehrenbacher has shown, was Lincoln's need to distinguish his position from that of Douglas in the wake of the latter's break with the Buchanan administration when it proposed to admit Kansas to the Union as a slave state under the Lecompton constitution, a charter that clearly did not reflect the will of the people of the territory. For some Eastern Republicans, this action made Douglas a de facto opponent of the expansion of slavery and perhaps worthy of Republican support. By making statements in the "House Divided" speech that Douglas could never assent to, and also contending, somewhat demagogically, that Douglas was one of the conspirators who were seeking to nationalize slavery, Lincoln foreclosed the possibility that Republicans might cooperate with Douglas in some kind of anti-Lecompton coalition. He represented Douglas's indifference as to whether slavery was voted up or down in a fair election in a territory exercising "popular sovereignty" as a covert way of supporting slavery's expansion, if not to Kansas then somewhere else. In the process of calling attention to Douglas's amorality, Lincoln affirmed the moral core of the Republican commitment to free soil.[48]

A final question about the speech is whether Lincoln was right or even sincere when he warned that another Supreme Court decision was in the offing that would make slavery legal not only in the territories but in all of the states. Although the prospect might seem farfetched, we should recall that few people had anticipated the Dred Scott decision, which had made the extreme Southern position on slavery in the territories the law of the land and pulled the rug out from under Douglas's panacea of "popular sovereignty." If slaves were to be considered simply property like any other physical possession, it was not inconceivable that a pro-Southern Supreme Court would rule that owners of slaves be granted the same right as the owners of livestock, household furniture, or gold bullion to transport such property from one state to another. To Lincoln's way of thinking, this was a real possibility against which the public in the free states had to be warned.

The seven Great Debates between Lincoln and Douglas, which were the highlights of the senatorial race of 1858, mostly repeated positions that the candidates had already taken. Douglas's strategy was to represent Lincoln as an abolitionist and racial egalitarian. In the first speech of the first debate, Douglas claimed that "Mr. Lincoln and the Black Republican party" were "in favor of citizenship for the negro." As for himself, he was "opposed to negro citizenship in any and every form. (Cheers.) I believe this government was made by white men for the benefit of white men and their posterity forever, and I am in favor of confining citizenship to white men, men of European birth and descent, instead of conferring it on negroes, Indians, and other inferior races." Douglas went on to reject the opinion of

Lincoln and "all the little abolition orators" that black equality is affirmed in the Declaration of Independence. In Douglas's opinion, "all men" meant all white men; it did not include blacks or other "inferior races."[49] Lincoln's rejoinder to the allegation that he favored black citizenship was to claim for blacks the natural rights to life, liberty, and the pursuit of happiness as set forth in the Declaration, but then to deny that this meant they could be equal to whites and eligible for the rights of citizenship. Lincoln reformulated for the occasion the basic point that he had made in the Peoria speech: "I agree with Judge Douglas that [the Negro] is not my equal in many respects—certainly not in color, perhaps not in moral or intellectual endowment. But in the right to eat the bread, without leave of anybody else, which his own hand earns, he is my equal and the equal of Judge Douglas, and the equal of every living man."[50]

Once again, one is struck by Lincoln's minimalist and somewhat impoverished conception of the rights to life, liberty, and the pursuit of happiness. It boiled down to the right not to be a slave and to acquire and possess property. But history has demonstrated that without civil and political rights, African Americans did not have what Lincoln later called "an unfettered start, and a fair chance, in the race of life."[51] Clearly the opportunities to acquire property that were offered to blacks in antebellum Illinois scarcely equaled those enjoyed by whites. How, for example, could blacks exercise their right to property without the protections provided by a legal system to which they had very limited access? Lincoln made it clear in the fourth debate that blacks were entirely at the mercy of all-white state legislatures: "I do not understand that there is any place where an alteration of the social and political relations of the negro and the white man can be made except in the state legislature—not in the Congress of the United States."[52]

Lincoln's strongest endorsement of the discriminatory "black laws" of Illinois also came in the fourth debate, which took place in Charleston in the southern part of the state. Some historians have viewed the white supremacist tenor of this speech as a pandering to the particularly strong racist sentiments that prevailed in southern Illinois. Douglas accused Lincoln of speaking one way in the northern part of the state, where public opinion was more tolerant of blacks, and taking another tack entirely in "Egypt" (as southern Illinois was called because its principal town was Cairo). It is true that Lincoln did not stress his opposition to black rights so candidly in the other debates, but he did not say anything in other debates that contradicted the Charleston statement.[53] Lincoln began by reporting that he had been asked if he "was really in favor of producing a perfect equality between the negroes and white people." His answer was strongly in the negative: "I am not, nor ever have been in favor of bringing about in any way the equality of the white and black races, (Applause)—I am not nor ever have been in favor of making voters or jurors of negroes, nor of qualifying them to hold office, nor to intermarry with white people." The justification for this discrimination was "that there is a physical difference between the white and black races that will for ever forbid the two races from living together on terms of social and political equality." But this fact of life did not justify their enslavement. At this point, Lincoln repeated his old line that people should not think that "because I do not want a negro woman for a slave I must necessarily want her for a wife."[54]

These words from the Charleston debate are the ones most often quoted by those who characterize Lincoln as a fervent, dyed-in-the-wool racist, despite his moral condemnation of slavery. His antislavery credentials might also be questioned on the grounds that he did not propose to do anything about the South's "peculiar institution" except prevent its expansion. As he put it in the first debate, the containment of slavery would make it possible for the institution "to be let alone for a hundred years, if it should live so long, yet it would be going out of existence in the way best for both the black and white races. [Great Cheering.]"[55] Once again, we can see a yawning gap between Lincoln and the abolitionists, who favored immediate emancipation and racial equality. In the seventh debate, Lincoln made clear his attitude toward antislavery radicals: "If there be a man among us who is so impatient of [slavery] as a wrong as to disregard its actual presence among us and the difficulty of getting rid of it suddenly in a satisfactory way, and to disregard the constitutional obligations thrown about it, that man is misplaced if he is on our platform. We disclaim sympathy for him in practical action."[56]

Nevertheless, Lincoln's professed attitudes toward slavery and race differed significantly from those of Douglas. Lincoln was not the first to raise the issue of black equality and would probably not have dwelt on it had Douglas not forced him to. As it was, Lincoln's assertion of black inequality usually had a somewhat tentative or qualified aspect that differed from Douglas's dogmatic contention that blacks were subhuman creatures. A black was "certainly" not his equal in "color, perhaps not in moral or intellectual endowment." Douglas and other negrophobic racists would not have said "perhaps" but would have trumpeted this alleged inferiority of capabilities with absolute conviction. And what precisely did Lincoln mean by inferiority of "color"? What exactly was "the physical difference" that "would forever forbid the two races living together on terms of social and political equality"? One possible interpretation is that Lincoln believed in racial incompatibility but regarded the question of whether blacks and whites were innately and permanently unequal in capabilities as an open one. Simply because blacks would always look different in ways that whites found distasteful, prejudice and discrimination against them were inevitable.

One might derive a theoretical understanding of such an attitude toward racial difference from the Dutch sociologist H. Hoetink, who has argued that the dominant groups in racially "segmented societies" possess "somatic norm images," or conceptions of what people are supposed to look like, that may lead to a disdainful and exclusionary attitude toward groups that deviate from the norm in readily identifiable ways.[57] Whether Lincoln partook of this aesthetic racism based on color difference, or merely recognized it as the inevitable and ineradicable sentiment of most white Americans, is difficult to determine. But one way or the other, it lay behind his persistent interest in colonization, which surfaced once again in the fifth debate when he quoted Henry Clay to the effect that colonization would help prepare the way for emancipation and that attacking it on those grounds, as proslavery extremists were wont to do, was treason to the Founding Fathers and the Declaration of Independence.[58]

On the rightness or wrongness of slavery as an institution, the differences between Lincoln and Douglas were more obvious and straightforward. For Douglas, there was nothing wrong with slavery provided that it was the will of the (white) people to have it and that its victims were black. Lincoln's private attitude toward slavery came out most strongly in an 1855 letter to his old friend Joshua Speed, a Kentuckian who owned slaves, in which he recalled seeing shackled slaves on a steamboat trip from Louisville to St. Louis. "The sight was a continual torment to me," Lincoln recalled, and he asked Speed to "appreciate how much the great body of the Northern people do crucify their feelings in order to maintain their loyalty to the constitution and the Union."[59] In the sixth debate, Lincoln characterized the controversy over slavery as a starkly moral conflict: "The difference of opinion reduced to its lowest terms, is no other than the difference between the men who think slavery wrong and those who do not think it wrong. The Republican party think it wrong—we think it is a moral, a social and a political wrong." As usual, Lincoln conceded that the Constitution precluded direct action against slavery where it already existed, except perhaps in the District of Columbia. But this did not prevent him from taking a strong moral stand against slavery where in his view it was not protected by the Constitution, namely in the territories.[60] As Don E. Fehrenbacher has convincingly argued, Lincoln deserves a great deal of credit for keeping the Republican Party focused on the immorality of slavery. In ways that one could not foresee at the time, the promulgation of this judgment would make it easier for the federal government to act against slavery when circumstances permitted it to do so in 1862 and 1863 than would otherwise have been the case.[61]

Lincoln of course lost the senatorial election to Douglas in the gerrymandered state legislature, despite winning the popular vote. But he emerged as a major figure in the Republican Party and campaigned for the party in the off-year elections of 1859. In Ohio, again on the heels of Douglas who was stumping the state for the Democrats, Lincoln denounced Douglas's belief in the sub-humanity of blacks more forthrightly than he had done in Illinois, charging that his rival had demoted the black man "from the rank of a man to that of a brute." Douglas's statement that he was for the Negro against the crocodile but for the white man against the Negro was interpreted by Lincoln as meaning that "as the negro may rightfully treat the crocodile as a beast or a reptile, so the white man may rightfully treat the negro as a beast or a reptile."[62]

In February 1860 Lincoln gave a major speech at Cooper Institute in New York City, in which he set forth his fully developed prewar view of the slavery issue. Much of the address was devoted to examining the views of the Founding Fathers on the question of whether slavery should be allowed to expand. Lincoln concluded on the basis of substantial research that thirty-six of those intimately involved in the founding of the nation, out of a total of thirty-nine whose opinions could be determined or surmised, believed that the federal government had the power and the responsibility to restrict the spread of slavery.[63] "As those fathers marked it," Lincoln concluded from his investigation, "let it again be marked, as an evil not to be extended, but to be tolerated and protected only because of and so far as its actual presence among us makes that toleration and protection a ne-

cessity."[64] This in brief is the platform on which the Republican Party would run in 1860, propelling Lincoln into the White House and precipitating a secession and civil war.

What can we conclude in general about Lincoln's views on slavery and race between 1854 and 1860, and how they might have been affected by the political context in which he operated? First of all, there is no reason to doubt the sincerity of Lincoln's numerous statements, public and private, to the effect that he detested slavery and opposed it in principle.[65] Nevertheless, as he also pointed out on many occasions, his reverence for the Constitution and the rule of law precluded any action beyond limiting slavery's expansion. Lincoln was an ambitious politician, but it would be the height of cynicism not to take him at his word on these matters. His very success as a politician can be attributed in large part to his power in articulating these antislavery ideas and values, which he could not have done nearly so effectively had he not believed in them himself.

The question of Lincoln's specifically racial attitudes during his Illinois years presents a more difficult problem of interpretation. If we take him at his word on race as well as on slavery, he comes across as a convinced believer in white supremacy. Consequently, the case of those who characterize him as a hard-core racist during this period would appear to be stronger than that of those who see him as a covert proponent of racial equality. But the possibility remains that it was political expediency more than settled conviction that produced the statements that we now find blatantly racist. As we have seen, Illinois was probably the most negrophobic Northern state. When he was accused of advocating the social and political equality of the races, Lincoln responded in the manner that political necessity clearly required. His strongest assertions of racial inequality or incompatibility came when he was under attack from Douglas, who sought to make him look like a member of the highly unpopular abolitionist minority. Lincoln would not have had a chance in the 1858 election if he had not publicly conformed to the white supremacist consensus among the voters. Still, it remains likely that Lincoln shared that consensus view, at least to some extent. Although he evinced no hatred of blacks and empathized with the suffering of the slaves, he also gave little indication, even in private, that he was sensitive or sympathetic to the plight of free African Americans in the North.

A standard by which Lincoln might be judged—one that would not remove him from the realm of what was possible in his historical context (and in effect apply a modern test for "political correctness")—is the behavior of other Republicans at the time. Eric Foner in his pathbreaking study of the ideology of the Republican Party in the 1850s maintains that "even in the West, the stronghold of racism, a majority of Republicans were ready to give some recognition to Negro rights, and the party strenuously opposed Democratic efforts to enact new anti-black legislation." Foner also notes that "a majority of Illinois Republicans" tried unsuccessfully to "repeal that state's black laws in 1857" and in 1859 "voted to allow Negroes to testify in court and attend the public schools."[66] Lincoln, it seems, was among the minority of Republicans who failed to support these efforts to extend minimal civil rights to blacks. In contemporary terms, we might say that he was somewhat to the right of center on these issues within his own party. We have already noted his refusal in 1858 to sign a petition supporting legislation that would give blacks the right to testify in court. Lincoln's hands-off policy when it came to the extension of black rights can be partly explained in the light of his geographic location in the center of the state and the fact that he was running statewide in 1858. The more radical Republicans, as typified by Representative Owen Lovejoy, tended to be concentrated in northern Illinois and as officeholders were responsible only to a local electorate.

An examination of Lincoln's thought and actions before 1860 points to the conclusion that he was genuinely antislavery, but in a way that did not provide the basis for any action that would violate a rather strict construction of the Constitution. On the question of racial differences and policies, the prewar Lincoln was clearly a white supremacist, but of a relatively passive or reactive kind as compared with his Democratic opponents. It is not true, as is sometimes asserted, that there are no degrees of racism—that one is either a racist or one is not. There is actually a spectrum of attitudes that might legitimately be labeled "racist," ranging from genocidal hatred of "the other" to mere conformity to the practices of a racially stratified society. Although political necessity forced him to endorse those practices publicly, Lincoln's personal attitudes, to the extent that we can determine them, were much closer to racism as conformity than to racism as pathology.[67]

In the next chapter I will consider whether presiding over a war in which "military necessity" dictated the emancipation of slaves and their use as soldiers led to a significant change in Lincoln's attitude toward blacks and their future in America.

3

Becoming an Emancipator:
The War Years

AS THE HISTORIAN David Potter wrote more than forty years ago, Lincoln "always regarded the perpetuation of the Union as more important than the abolition of slavery."[1] Although recent historians have tended to give greater weight to Lincoln's antislavery convictions than some of their predecessors, they have not been able to reverse the priorities. Lincoln made it clear early in the war that he would have saved the Union without abolishing slavery if that had been possible. His sincere hatred of the South's "peculiar institution" is not in doubt, however. In a letter written in 1864, he succinctly explained the process that had led him to become an emancipator: "I am naturally anti-slavery. If slavery is not wrong, nothing is wrong. . . . And yet I never understood that the Presidency conferred on me the unrestricted right to act officially upon this judgment or feeling." It was only when the necessities of a war to preserve the Union and the Constitution required it that Lincoln proclaimed emancipation, having been "driven to the alternative of either surrendering the Union, and with it, the Constitution, or of laying strong hand upon the colored element. I chose the latter."[2] This in brief is how Lincoln became an emancipator, but his account does not fully explain why emancipation took the form that it did or what it connoted about his attitude toward the rights of blacks when they were no longer slaves.

For Lincoln, the main aim of the war was to preserve a form of government and the ideas underlying it. In a speech he gave in Philadelphia on his way to being inaugurated in Washington in 1861, he paid homage to the Declaration of Independence for "giving liberty not just to the people of this country, but hope to the world for all future time. (Great applause.) It was that which gave promise that in due time the weights should be lifted from the shoulders of all men, and that *all* should have an equal chance."[3] Lincoln went on to suggest that the Union would not be worth saving if it did not embody the sentiments expressed in the Declaration.

Lincoln's conception of how the Declaration related to the Constitution came out most fully in an undated "Fragment on the Constitution and the Union" that was probably written when he was president-elect and giving thought to his inaugural address. In this statement he compared the Declaration to "an apple of gold" and the Constitution to a *"picture of silver"* that framed it: "The picture was made not to *conceal,* or *destroy* the apple, but to *adorn* and *preserve it.*"[4] In other words, the Declaration was the soul of the Constitution. As we have already seen, however, Lincoln's conception of the rights to "life, liberty, and the pursuit of happiness" did not mandate the civil and political equality of blacks. It did clash with the principle of slavery, but the Constitution protected the institution in a section of the country because of the rights it granted to the states. In the United States that Lincoln addressed in his First Inaugural of March 1861, abolition seemed a very distant prospect, and the new president indicated his willingness to accept a proposed "unamendable" amendment to the Constitution that would explicitly forbid the federal government from ever interfering with slavery in the states.[5]

At the outset of the war, Lincoln defined the issue as a test of whether a democratic government could maintain itself against the refusal of a minority to accept the verdict of a constitutional majority—whether it could survive a major internal challenge, such as that represented by the secession of the South. Lincoln put his notion of what was at stake most strongly in his special message to Congress of July 4, 1861. The issue of the war, he announced, "embraces more than the fate of these United States. It presents to the whole family of man, the question of whether a constitutional republic, or a democracy—a government of the people, by the same people—can maintain its territorial integrity against its own domestic foes. . . . It forces us to ask: 'Is there in all republics this inherent and fatal weakness? Must a government, of necessity, be too *strong* for the liberties of its own people, or too *weak* to maintain its own existence?'"[6] Later in the same address Lincoln described the war for the Union as "a People's contest . . . a struggle for maintaining in the world, that form and substance of government, whose leading object is, to elevate the condition of men—to lift artificial weights from all shoulders—to clear the paths of laudable pursuit for all—to afford all, an unfettered start, and a fair chance in the race of life. Yielding to partial, and temporary departures, from necessity, this is the leading object of the government for whose existence we contend."[7]

With eloquence and conviction, Lincoln thus made the cause of the American Union into the worldwide cause of democracy and free labor. Slavery was admittedly incompatible with these ideals, but necessity required that it be tolerated as a "partial, and temporary" departure from them. Although it was a blemish and a source of embarrassment, it was not, it would seem, a fatal flaw that deprived the United States of its exemplary status as the world's premier democratic republic. Lincoln went on in the special message to Congress to make it clear that suppression of the rebellion would not change the relation of the states to the federal government, which meant that those states wishing to retain slavery would still be free to do so.

At this point, in the early stages of the conflict, Lincoln evinced little or no concern for the rights and destiny of African Americans. In fact, if some reports of his private comments can be believed, he could speak of blacks in a callous or jocular fashion that conveyed a disinclination to pay attention to their plight and potential role in the struggle to save the Union. After his election but before he took office, he reportedly told a group of men a story about a successful candidate for the office of justice of the peace in Kentucky who found that the first case that came before him "was criminal prosecution for the abuse of Negro slaves"—a complex and murky affair for which he could find no adequate precedents. "'I will be damned,'" he cried out angrily, "'if I don't feel almost sorry for being elected when the niggers is the first thing I have to attend to.'"[8] In September 1861, after Lincoln had requested General John C. Frémont to refrain from using martial law to emancipate the slaves of Missouri, he received Frémont's wife, who brought a letter explaining her husband's reluctance to comply with the president's wishes. According to Jesse Benton Frémont, Lincoln responded testily and dogmatically: "The general should never have dragged the Negro into the war. It is a war for a great national object, and the Negro has nothing to do with it."[9]

Whether or not Lincoln spoke these exact words, his actions during the first year or so of the war revealed a strong aversion to moving against slavery through military action. He formally overruled Frémont's emancipation policy and soon relieved him of his command.

When in May 1862 General David Hunter attempted to use martial law to free the slaves in coastal South Carolina, Georgia, and Florida and to recruit blacks as soldiers, the president voided the action, claiming for himself rather than his generals the prerogative of invoking military necessity for interfering with slavery.[10] Whatever his personal feelings about slavery may have been, Lincoln had what he considered strong practical reasons for restraining antislavery action. In a letter explaining why he countermanded Frémont, he stressed the necessity of maintaining the loyalty of the slave states that had remained in the Union, especially Kentucky. "I think to lose Kentucky," he wrote to his friend Orville H. Browning, "is nearly to lose the whole game. Kentucky gone, we can not hold Missouri, nor as I think, Maryland."[11]

But there was a deeper reason for Lincoln's unwillingness to bring the slavery issue to the fore. As he indicated in his annual message to Congress in December 1861, he had been "anxious and careful" in the policies he adopted for "suppressing the insurrection" lest the conflict "degenerate into a violent and remorseless revolutionary struggle." For that reason, he "had thought it proper to keep the integrity of the Union prominent as the primary object of the contest."[12] Lincoln had long been fearful of popular passions or enthusiasms, as he had demonstrated many years before in his Lyceum Speech of 1838. He realized that direct threats to slavery aroused intense emotions among Southern whites and might also incite the slaves to rebellion. Of Southern origin himself, Lincoln could empathize with the anxieties and dangers faced by those who had found themselves, like his hero Henry Clay, dependent on an established institution which they disapproved of in principle but could see no practical, satisfactory means of eliminating.

At the same time that he was resisting efforts to free slaves through martial law, Lincoln was beginning to think seriously about other, less revolutionary ways of putting slavery more firmly "in course of ultimate extinction." In the same annual message to Congress in which he abjured revolutionary action, he noted that the slaves who had come into the possession of the federal government through the Confiscation Act of 1861 (because they were being employed directly in the service of the Confederacy) should be considered free and "must be provided for in some way." Since the Confiscation Act did not explicitly offer freedom, this decision can be considered Lincoln's first emancipatory act, but it was not unexpected or controversial. Given the views of Lincoln and other Republicans on the relationship of the federal government to slavery, it was almost inconceivable that the government would assume the direct ownership of confiscated slaves. Lincoln then suggested that the loyal slave states might be induced to emancipate their own slaves, provided that they were compensated by the federal government and that "steps be taken for colonizing both classes [those confiscated and those voluntarily freed by the border states] . . . at some place or places in a climate congenial to them."[13] Here was the first public indication of Lincoln's master plan for ending slavery in a non-revolutionary fashion—gradual, compensated emancipation followed by colonization of the freed people in a "congenial clime" outside the United States.[14]

On the same day in December 1861 when Lincoln first made his plan public, he gave a more detailed explanation of what he had in mind when he talked with his friend Orville Browning about "paying Delaware, Maryland, Kentucky, and Missouri $500 apiece for all the slaves they had according to the census of 1860, provided they adopted a system of gradual emancipation which would work the extinction of slavery in twenty years." He and Browning agreed that the plan should involve colonizing the freed blacks outside of the United States.[15] In the back of Lincoln's mind, in all likelihood, was the hope that putting such a program into operation in the loyal slave states would provide a basis for inducing the rebellious states to return to the Union without a loss of wealth and with their racial anxieties assuaged by the prospect of a reduction of the black population through subsidized colonization. In the proclamation revoking General Hunter's emancipation order in May 1862, Lincoln repeated his call to the states to adopt gradual, compensated emancipation so that "the change it contemplates will come gently as the dews of heaven, not rending or wrecking anything."[16]

The strength of Lincoln's commitment to a very gradual (as opposed to any sudden or disruptive) emancipation was revealed in his reaction to the congressional legislation that abolished slavery in the District of Columbia in April 1862. Although the owners were compensated and funds were appropriated for colonization, emancipation in this case was immediate rather than gradual, and Lincoln signed the bill with reluctance. According to Browning, he said "that he regretted the bill had been passed in its present form; that it should have been for gradual emancipation; that families would at once be deprived of cooks, stable

boys, etc., and they of their protectors without any provision for them."[17]

The first state that Lincoln tried to enlist in his program of gradual emancipation was Delaware, which
had so few slaves—a total of 1,800 in 1860—that it
was hard to imagine strong opposition to their being
purchased and freed by the federal government. In late
November 1861, Lincoln went so far as to draft a bill
to be presented to the Delaware state legislature providing for gradual, federally compensated emancipation.
Under its proposed terms, slavery would not be totally eliminated until 1893. But even in a state that had
no significant economic stake in slavery, the fear that
emancipated blacks would claim equal rights caused a
bill along the lines that Lincoln recommended to be
narrowly defeated.[18] Undaunted, Lincoln next turned
his attention to the border slave states as a whole. In
a message to Congress in March 1862, he called for a
joint resolution "resolving that the United States ought
to cooperate with any state which may adopt gradual
abolishment of slavery, giving to such state pecuniary
aid, to be used by each such states . . . to compensate
for the inconveniences public and private, produced by
such change of system." In the address proposing this

resolution, Lincoln argued that this action would make it less likely that the border states would be induced to join the Confederacy. As a general principle, he affirmed that "gradual, not sudden emancipation, is better for all." He also made it clear that he was not claiming any federal right "to interfere with slavery within state limits" and that "absolute control of the subject" remained in state hands; adoption of the gradual emancipation plan would be strictly voluntary.[19]

A passage in Lincoln's original draft of this message that was deleted from the final version followed his recognition of the right of the loyal slave states to deal as they pleased with slavery within their own borders. It revealed that as late as March 1862, Lincoln was still visualizing a restoration of the Union with slavery surviving but once again "in course of ultimate extinction." Fearful perhaps of arousing the hostility of those in the North who thought he was moving too slowly against slavery, he omitted the following passage: "Should the people of the insurgent districts now reject the councils of treason, revive loyal state governments, and again send Senators and Representatives to Congress, they would at once find themselves at peace, with no institution changed, and their just influence in the councils of the nation, fully re-established." In other words, the old

Union, or at least the Union before the passage of the Kansas-Nebraska Act had created the prospect of slavery's expansion, would be restored, along with the possibility that gradual, compensated emancipation could become a national policy. Here, once again, Lincoln's constitutional conservatism manifested itself. His proposal to make the offer to the border states was approved by Congress on April 10, 1862.[20]

Lincoln's campaign for compensated emancipation in the border states initially attracted substantial support in the North, but it soon came face-to-face with the obdurate refusal of the targeted states to cooperate. A majority of the congressional representatives of the loyal slave states voted against the resolution, arguing that it opened the way to federal action against slavery in the South. One by one, despite fervent direct appeals from the president, the border state legislatures spurned the proposal.[21] Lincoln's preferred plan for restoring the Union and gradually abolishing slavery without pecuniary loss to the owners was going nowhere. The apparent futility of gaining support for this moderate, non-revolutionary effort to phase out slavery, as well as the fact that the war was going badly (especially in the East, where McClellan's ambitious Peninsula campaign had foundered), created growing pressure from the Northern public for a direct assault on slavery in the rebellious Southern states. Emancipation was now being advocated not only by antislavery radicals on moral and humanitarian grounds, but also by some hard-headed Unionist conservatives who, without evincing any noticeable sympathy for blacks, saw it as a necessary or expedient contribution to the Northern war effort.[22]

By the summer of 1862 Lincoln himself had come around to this way of thinking. On July 22, 1862, he summoned his Cabinet and read to them a draft of a proclamation in which he declared that the slaves in areas still in rebellion against "the constitutional authority of the United States" on January 1, 1863, "shall then, thenceforward, and forever be free." His justification was that such an emancipation was "a fit and necessary military measure." It is noteworthy, however, that he combined this prospective general emancipation in areas under confederate control with a reiteration of his offer of "pecuniary aid" for states that would "adopt the gradual abolishment of slavery." He may well have been hoping against hope that at least some of the states in rebellion would return to the Union during the next six months in order to take him up on his offer.[23] As everyone knows, Secretary of State William Seward persuaded Lincoln and the Cabinet to hold off on issuing the proclamation until the Union had won a military victory, lest emancipation appear to the world like an act of desperation.

It was during the period between the time when the basic decision for emancipation had been made and September 22, when the Preliminary Proclamation was issued, that Lincoln's behavior has been viewed by some historians as evidence of his close-to-the-vest political shrewdness or deviousness in a good cause. Although he allegedly had already decided to free the slaves, he gave the impression that the matter was still under consideration. He was waiting, according to this interpretation, for a moment when an action that was bound to be controversial could be presented in a way calculated to gain maximum popular support. Responding in a public letter of August 22 to the editor Horace Greeley's criticism of his failure to strike a blow against slavery, Lincoln set forth his general stance on the relationship of his presidential authority to the question of emancipation. "My paramount object in this struggle is to save the Union," he wrote, "and is *not* either to save or destroy slavery. If I could save the Union without freeing *any* slave I would do it, and if I could save it by freeing *all* the slaves I would do it, and if I could save it by freeing some and leaving others alone, I would also do that." He ended the letter by distinguishing between his personal feelings and what his office required of him: "I have here stated my purpose according to my view of *official* duty; and I intend no modification of my oft-expressed *personal* wish that all men every where could be free."[24]

But was this really a deceptive or Machiavellian statement? It can more plausibly be read as a frank and honest avowal of what Lincoln considered his options to be. He made it clear that he had the authority to free slaves if that were necessary to save the Union. Thus he was preparing the way for public acceptance of the Preliminary Emancipation Proclamation, which came a month after his letter to Greeley. In a way, it incorporated two of the three possible courses of action that Lincoln laid out for Greeley. There was the admittedly remote possibility that the seceded states would agree to rejoin the Union before January 1, 1863, in which case the Union would be saved without freeing a single slave. In the more likely event that they remained in a state of rebellion, those slaves behind enemy lines would be declared free, but not those in areas under Union control. This would have meant that some slaves would be freed and others left alone. A general emancipation could not be proclaimed, Lincoln believed, because he lacked the constitutional authority to interfere with slavery in loyal or occupied areas where it existed under state law. In the Preliminary Proclamation he sketched out his plan for emancipation in slave states that were not in rebellion. He again announced his intention to ask Congress to appropriate funds to enable these border states, if they so desired, to initiate gradual, compensated emancipation, and to make it possible to "colonize people of African descent, with their consent, upon this continent or elsewhere."[25]

The official justification for the Emancipation Proclamation was "military necessity" in time of civil war. Despite the victory at Antietam, which repulsed the first Confederate effort to carry the war into the North, most of the South remained unconquered and, it must have seemed to many, unconquerable. The North was having difficulty putting enough men into the field, and fervent opponents of slavery were beginning to recommend the use of black troops. Lincoln was hesitant to use blacks as soldiers.[26] But by the time of the final Emancipation Proclamation, Northern manpower needs had become even more compelling, and the enlistment of blacks as soldiers was authorized. The pragmatic justifications for an emancipation policy were obvious: it would augment the forces trying to put down the rebellion, strike a body blow at a Southern economy dependent on slave labor, and gain the sympathy of foreign powers such as England and France, which in late 1862 seemed on the verge of recognizing the Confederacy.

But there was another important factor creating pressure for emancipation—the will of the slaves themselves to become free and actively contribute to the Northern war effort, once they realized that it could mean the end of slavery. From the beginning of hostilities, slaves had been running away from their masters and crossing over into Union lines. Early in the war some slaves had been returned to their owners, but the advantages of having them available, first as laborers and then as soldiers, soon became apparent. Before the Preliminary Emancipation Proclamation was promulgated, tens of thousands of slaves had in effect freed themselves from bondage and enlisted in the Union cause. In the words of Ira Berlin, they "were the prime movers in the emancipation drama, not the sole movers. Slaves set others in motion, including many who would never have moved if left to their own devices."[27] The question for us is whether Lincoln was among those who "would never have moved" if slaves had remained passive, docile laborers on Southern plantations rather than potential recruits to the invading Northern forces. As with any counterfactual proposition, no firm answer is possible. Lincoln made no mention of slave initiatives in either the draft proclamation of July 1862 or the Preliminary Proclamation issued in September. It seems likely that his aim was more to encourage the slaves to desert their masters than to take advantage of a *fait accompli*. According to Allen C. Guelzo, relatively few escaped slaves were under Union control in September 1862. It was not until the Emancipation Proclamation made it virtually certain that absconding slaves would become free men and women that the real flood took place.[28] A relatively safe conclusion would be that the original "contrabands" of the first year and a half of the war suggested to Lincoln that official emancipation would encourage more runaways, both weakening the Southern economy and augmenting the manpower available for service to the Union. If this was indeed Lincoln's intention, the results exceeded his expectations.

Lincoln's adoption of an emancipation policy in the last six months of 1862 did not deter him from promoting the colonization of blacks outside the United States as a solution to the acute race problem that he believed would arise if whites and freed blacks tried to coexist in the same society. On August 14, 1862, Lincoln summoned a representative group of African Americans to the White House in order to drum up black support for colonization. His much-publicized address provides the fullest rendition of his thinking about race relations. "You and we are different races," he told the delegation. "We have between us a broader difference than exists between any other two races. . . . This physical difference is a great disadvantage to us both, as I think your race suffer very greatly, many of them by living among us, while ours suffer from your presence." Whites suffered, he ungenerously observed, because without the black presence there would have been no Civil War. But enslaved blacks, Lincoln acknowledged, "are suffering the greatest wrong inflicted on any people." Even when freed, however, "you are yet far removed from being placed on equality with the white race . . . not a single man of your race is made the equal of a single man of ours." "It is better for us both therefore to be separated," he concluded. Lincoln then held up George Washington as an example of heroic sacrifice that blacks might emulate. During the Revolution, he "was engaged in benefiting *his race*." By thus racializing Washington's achievement, Lincoln implied that blacks could never hope to partake fully of American nationality.[29]

In his speculations about suitable destinations for colonized blacks Lincoln put great emphasis on the congeniality of climate, a calculus that reflected his racialist belief that whites and blacks were physically and psychologically adapted to different climatic conditions. In his White House speech to the black delegation, he proposed Central America as a destination, because of "the similarity of climate to your native land [Africa]—thus being suited to your physical condition." He ruled out Liberia as the main destination, partly because many African Americans found West Africa too remote from the land of their nativity. Furthermore, Liberia was not on the main shipping lines and sending blacks there would be very expensive, quickly exhausting the $600,000 Congress had appropriated to subsidize colonization.[30]

In his subsequent efforts to find suitable locations for African American colonies, Lincoln concentrated on Central America and the Caribbean. The place that Lincoln found most promising was Chiriqui, a province of Colombia, which is now part of Panama. On September 11, 1862, he ordered that a contract be signed with a group of United States speculators who claimed title to land in the province and maintained that its coal deposits would provide a livelihood for the emigrants. But the Chiriqui Improvement Company, as it turned out, lacked a clear title to the land and exaggerated its economic potential. What finally doomed the project were the protests of Central American states against the establishment of such a colony in their neighborhood. The Lincoln administration next attempted to induce some of the European countries with colonies in Central America and the Caribbean to receive African American immigrants. Some tentative negotiations took place, but in the end they came to nothing. Finally, Lincoln's search for a place to which to send African Americans came to focus on an island off the coast of Haiti which had been leased by an American entrepreneur. In April 1863, 463 blacks were actually sent to the island. But conditions there turned out to be unbearable. Economic opportunity was very limited, and disease took a heavy toll. Those who survived (85 had died, mostly from malaria) had to be rescued and brought back to the United States after eleven months.[31]

Lincoln's advocacy of colonization, though yielding few tangible results, was an integral part of his persistent effort to persuade the border slave states to embrace gradual, compensated emancipation. In addition to being presented directly to representatives of those states, the proposal was inserted in the Preliminary Emancipation Proclamation, with the implication that the states of the Confederacy could take advantage of it in the unlikely event that they ceased their rebellion before January 1. A Cabinet meeting of September 24, 1862, addressed the issue of colonization, and, according to the recollection of Secretary of the Navy Gideon Welles, Lincoln justified black expatriation in the face of impending emancipation as a way to "provide an asylum . . . for a race that could never be our equals." But as always, he made it clear that colonization should be voluntary.[32] In his annual message to Congress on December 1, 1862, just one month before the final Emancipation Proclamation, Lincoln proposed three constitutional amendments. The first offered compensation to any state adopting gradual emancipation to be completed by 1900. A state "reintroducing or tolerating slavery" would forfeit the compensation. The second declared slaves "who shall have enjoyed actual freedom by the chances of the war" to be "forever free," but authorized compensating their owners if they had not been disloyal. The third proposed that "Congress may appropriate money, and otherwise provide, for colonizing free colored persons, with their own consent, at any place or places outside the United States."[33]

Historians have been puzzled by the exact relationship of these proposed amendments to the impending Emancipation Proclamation. An obvious difference is that the former would change the fundamental law of the land to promote the gradual abolition of slavery, while the latter was an act of "military necessity," which might cease to have an effect when hostilities ended. The fact that the amendments permitted slavery to last almost forty more years and even raised the possibility of a state reintroducing it would seem to depart radically from the spirit of the Proclamation. The offer of compensation did not specify only loyal states, but Lincoln could hardly have imagined that the rebellious states would return to the Union within the next month. The provision that those slaves enjoying "actual freedom by the chances of war" would be permanently free might not apply to all those potentially liberated by the Proclamation of January 1, but only to those who managed to cross over into Union lines while the war was still going on. (We know that most slaves in the former Confederacy did not enjoy "actual freedom" when the war ended in 1865.) Could Lincoln have had in mind the possibility of some kind of negotiated settlement to restore the Union, which, even after the final Proclamation, would allow Southern states to return to the Union and retain those slaves still in their possession until 1900? His strong conviction that there was a suppressed Unionism among Southern whites that, under the right circumstances, could be brought to the fore, might have inspired such hopes or expectations.

The least ambiguous of the amendments was the one providing for subsidized voluntary colonization. But in the annual message Lincoln did not so much stress the urgency of this proposal as attempt to allay the Northern racial fears aroused by the prospect of a general emancipation with only very gradual and limited colonization. "I cannot make it better known than it already is that I strongly favor colonization," he pointed out. But he went on to say that "there is an objection urged against free colored persons remaining in the country, which is largely imaginary, if not sometimes malicious." Free blacks, he asserted, would not offer more competition with white labor than enslaved blacks. "With deportation, even to a limited extent, enhanced wages to white labor is mathematically certain. . . . Reduce the supply of black labor by colonizing the black laborer out of the country, and by precisely so much, you increase the demand for and wages of white labor." Most of those emancipated would, he predicted, remain in the South receiving wages for working for their former masters—now that it was no longer necessary to go North to attain freedom—"till new homes for them can be found in congenial climes."[34]

Lincoln concluded his discussion of why the North had no reason to fear a large influx of blacks with a startling statement, which has for the most part been overlooked by historians: "And in any event, cannot the north decide for itself, whether to receive them?" This question suggests that Lincoln's conception of the status of those freed by the war would be similar to, if not identical with, that of the "free Negroes" of the antebellum period. States would apparently retain the right to enact "black laws" like those still in effect in Illinois, which would include the right to exclude black migrants entirely.[35]

Addressing Congress on the eve of the Emancipation Proclamation, Lincoln had not given up on colonization as a long-term solution to the American race problem; he simply recognized that large numbers of African Americans were going to be emancipated well before provisions could be made for their emigration. But some historians have seen his conspicuous advocacy of colonization as insincere—as a device or ploy to make emancipation more palatable to a racist Northern electorate, the theory being that people would be more likely to countenance freeing the slaves if they assumed that the black presence in the United States was only temporary.[36] It is possible that some such political calculation was involved in Lincoln's colonizationism, but no direct evidence has been offered to support this hypothesis. It is just as likely, if not more so, that colonizationist rhetoric exacerbated white prejudice and impeded the cause of emancipation because of its emphasis, as in Lincoln's well-publicized speech to the black delegation, on the impossibility of racial equality within the United States. One could easily conclude, even if Lincoln did not, that retaining slavery would guarantee white supremacy better than a costly and problematic expatriation of blacks. The contrary, and arguably more plausible, assumption of abolitionists and antislavery radicals was that progress toward emancipation was dependent on an increasing acceptance among whites of racial equality in both theory and practice.

If Lincoln anticipated that his full program of gradual, compensated emancipation followed by subsidized colonization would go down well with the public and with Congress, he was sadly mistaken. The enterprise promised to be enormously expensive, and partly for that reason it attracted very little support, despite Lincoln's contention that it would hasten the end of the war and thus save money in the long run. The proposed constitutional amendments were scarcely even considered by Congress. In early 1863 all attention was focused on the effect of the Emancipation Proclamation, which really did promise to shorten the war. Given this lack of general enthusiasm for his scheme, it seems more likely that Lincoln's advocacy of compensated emancipation and colonization was a matter of conviction rather than political expediency.[37] Until the war was virtually over, Lincoln held on to the belief that one could shorten the war by offering Southern slaveowners compensation in return for their rejoining the Union. He tentatively offered such a proposal as his one concession to Confederate emissaries at a discussion of peace terms on a steamer off Hampton Roads, Virginia, in February 1865. A probable reason for Lincoln's persistent advocacy of compensation was a hope that paying money to slaveholders would lessen their resistance to reconstruction and reduce the urge to engage in guerrilla warfare against the Union occupiers. But when he brought up his proposal at a Cabinet meeting shortly after the conference, it encountered unanimous opposition, and he was persuaded to drop it.[38]

Lincoln did cease advocating colonization after he issued the final Emancipation Proclamation. His secretary John Hay reported in his diary on July 1, 1864, that he was "glad the President has sloughed off that idea of colonization," which Hay himself had always considered "a hideous and barbarous humbug."[39] It is likely that Lincoln stopped being a colonizationist a year or so earlier than Hay's report. In any case, his last public endorsement of the plan was in the December 1862 address to Congress. Why did Lincoln change his mind about the desirability of a government-sponsored and subsidized emigration of black Americans? An obvious reason was the one that Hay emphasized in his diary entry—the dismal failure of the Chiriqui and Haiti projects. But the change may also have reflected a transformation of Lincoln's basic attitude toward blacks and his conception of their future in American society. Once large numbers of blacks were enlisted in the Union army, as the result of a provision in the Emancipation Proclamation, their status was bound to change. Many former enthusiasts for colonization abandoned the cause in 1863 on the grounds that you cannot ask someone to fight for a country without acknowledging his right to live in it. A well-established tradition in republican thought was that bearing arms and citizenship went together.[40] Although he made no public admission of his change of heart, Lincoln, it appears, was one of the converts.

Before blacks actually went into battle, Lincoln was skeptical about their military potential. In the summer of 1862 he reportedly told a group of senators that he opposed arming blacks on the grounds that their weapons would quickly "be turned against us."[41] Shortly before he issued the Preliminary Emancipation Proclamation, he expressed a similar anxiety—his fear that "if we were to arm them . . . in a few weeks the arms would be in the hands of the rebels," implying that blacks would drop their weapons and run or abjectly surrender at the first sign of combat.[42] But once blacks proved themselves under fire in June and July of 1863, fighting heroically at Port Hudson and Milliken's Bend on the lower Mississippi and at Fort Wagner in South Carolina, Lincoln recognized their enormous potential value to the Union cause. In August 1863, he wrote to General Grant in support of "raising colored troops," describing them as a "resource which, if vigorously applied now, will soon close the contest."[43] In the same month, he went into the subject more fully in a public letter to a conservative Chicago Unionist who opposed emancipation and the use of blacks as soldiers. Lincoln countered that some of his generals believed that these policies "constitute the heaviest blow yet dealt to the rebellion." He then paid eloquent tribute to "blacks in blue." When the war was over and the Union saved, "there will be some black men who can remember that, with silent tongue, and clenched teeth, and steady eye, and well-poised bayonet, they have helped mankind to this great consummation; while, I fear, there will be some white ones, unable to forget that, with malignant heart and deceitful speech, they have strove to hinder it."[44]

On the question of whether black soldiers should be granted rights and privileges equal to those of whites under arms, Lincoln thought he had to tread carefully lest he provoke a white supremacist backlash. In his first meeting with the great black abolitionist Frederick Douglass on August 10, 1863, Lincoln had to deal with the criticism that blacks in the army were not receiving equal treatment and benefits. (They were, for example, paid less, denied officer commissions, and in the absence, as yet, of a threat of Union retaliation, they risked enslavement or execution if captured by the Confederates.) Lincoln's response to Douglass's call for a more egalitarian policy, the latter recalled, was that "the country was not ready for it," and "preparatory work" had to be done before enhancing the status of black troops. Despite the recent evidence of black heroism and commitment to the Northern cause, it remained true that "the colored man throughout his country was a despised man, a hated man." If Lincoln were to proclaim that the blacks in the military had to be treated as equals, "all the hatred which is poured on the head of the Negro would be visited on his administration."[45] Clearly, however, Lincoln's personal view of African Americans' capabilities had become more favorable as a result of their military achievements.

Lincoln's commitment to emancipating all slaves became evident in 1863 and 1864. He induced the border slave states of Maryland and Missouri and the reconstructed state of Louisiana to abolish slavery and made the acceptance of emancipation a condition of the amnesty for Southerners who returned to the fold under the terms of the Proclamation of Amnesty and Reconstruction that he issued on December 8, 1863. Finally, Lincoln supported, and saw included in the Republican platform of 1864, the proposal to abolish slavery throughout the nation by constitutional amendment. After his reelection he played a crucial role in winning congressional approval of the Thirteenth Amendment.

Before 1864, he had been a cautious, somewhat reluctant emancipator—certainly no advocate of an immediate, uncompensated emancipation without a link to colonization, which was the abolitionist's dream. But the fulfillment of that dream was what he ended up presiding over. Lincoln was thus able to realize his long-standing hope of extinguishing slavery and thereby earned and deserved the title of Great Emancipator.

But a troubling question remains. Did Lincoln, as some historians have contended, go beyond abolition without colonization to endorse civil and political equality for blacks? Did he move decisively beyond the position implied in the December 1862 Annual Message to Congress that freed Southern blacks could have the same inferior social and political status to which Northern free blacks had been relegated before the war? Whether Lincoln ever went beyond being an anti-slavery white supremacist to become a true egalitarian—like the abolitionists and Radical Republicans—is a question that is difficult to resolve because of the paucity of evidence directly bearing on it and because of the fact that Lincoln's thinking about race may have been in flux at the time of his assassination.

The strongest evidence that Lincoln was moving in the direction of greater civil and political rights for blacks comes from his advocacy of a qualified right to suffrage for African Americans in Louisiana. On March 13, 1864, he wrote to the new Unionist governor, Michael Hahn, to offer some advice on the constitution that was about to be drawn up by a convention of loyal white Louisianans. "I barely suggest for your private consideration," the letter said, "whether some of the colored people may not be let in—as, for instance, the very intelligent and especially those who have fought gallantly in our ranks."[46] But the convention did not extend the suffrage to blacks; the most that it was willing to do was grant the legislature the right to integrate the electorate if and when it decided to do so. Lincoln's first public affirmation of a qualified black suffrage came in his speech of April 11, 1865, on Reconstruction, the last public speech he made before he was assassinated. His remarks came in response to the opposition of Radical Republicans to his proposal to readmit Louisiana to the Union under the constitution of 1864. It was "unsatisfactory to some," he noted, "that the electoral franchise is not given to the Colored man. I would myself prefer that it were now conferred on the very intelligent, and on those who serve our cause as soldiers." Although imperfect, the Louisiana constitution was a step forward and could be improved in the future.[47]

In the minds of some historians, Lincoln's preference for a limited black suffrage in the reconstructed Southern states is evidence that he was moving closer to the congressional Radicals with whom he quarreled throughout the war about the timing and extent of emancipation. But it was indicative of persisting differences that Lincoln continued to rely on the states to determine the civil and political rights of blacks. Recognition of the right of blacks to be free was the only condition that Lincoln would require before a state could be readmitted to the Union. The Radicals, on the other hand, would impose further requirements for readmission, such as civil and political equality for blacks. There is no indication that the war and emancipation had changed the opinion Lincoln had expressed in the debates with Douglas in 1858: "I do not understand there is any place where an alteration of the social and political relations of the negro and the white man can be made except in the State Legislature—not in the Congress of the United States."[48] Lincoln's failure to require black suffrage as a condition for readmission to the Union, as he had imposed acceptance of the Emancipation Proclamation, reflected his belief that the Southern white Unionists should be the principal agents for bringing the seceded states back into normal relations with the states that had never left the Union. Whatever rights blacks might acquire in the reconstructed states, beyond the right not to be slaves, would be those that the whites who had sworn loyalty to the Union were willing to grant them.[49] The difference between Lincoln's basic view of the reconstruction process and who should be empowered to carry it out and the position of a majority of his own party in Congress, who saw blacks as key contributors, was never reconciled.

Dissatisfied by the leniency or permissiveness of the presidential reconstruction policy, Congress tried to take matters into its own hands. The Wade-Davis bill, passed on July 2, 1864, sought to establish more stringent conditions for restoration of the Union. Whereas Lincoln had required that only 10 percent of a state's population take an oath of loyalty to the Union before the reconstruction process could begin, Congress upped the ante to 50 percent and added other requirements. (It did not, however, mandate black suffrage.) Unlike Lincoln, who favored a quick and easy reconstruction, the congressional majority wanted to delay the process until it was certain that a majority of Southerners had embraced the Union fervently and unconditionally. When the bill reached the president as Congress went out of session, he pocket-vetoed it, being loath to see the efforts he had made to begin the process of reconstruction in Louisiana and also Arkansas come to naught. In a proclamation defending his veto, he described his policy as one that avoided being "inflexibly committed to any single plan of restoration." Any state that chose to do so could adopt the Wade-Davis formula.[50] Lincoln realized that his action would not improve his relations with a Congress now dominated by Radical Republicans. When asked about how his veto would affect his relations with the Radicals, he replied, according to John Hay, "They have never been friendly to me, and I don't know that this will make any special difference as to that."[51]

Differences on black civil and political rights came to the fore in a more clear-cut way when Congress attempted to pass another reconstruction bill when it reconvened in December 1864. In its original version, the bill, introduced by Representative James Ashley of Ohio, made blacks eligible to vote and serve on juries under the temporary governments to be established before readmission to the Union. According to John Hay, Lincoln found much of the bill acceptable, but not the provision for black political and civil rights (which was eventually dropped; what was left of the bill became part of a joint resolution submitting the Thirteenth Amendment to the states for ratification).[52] According to the recollections of his old friend Ward Lamon, Lincoln felt quite strongly that blacks were not ready for the degree of equality that was envisioned in the original Ashley bill. "While I am in favor of freedom to all of God's human creatures," he reportedly told Lamon, ". . . I am not in favor of unlimited social equality. . . . The question of universal suffrage for the freedman in his unprepared state is one of doubtful propriety."[53]

The view of some historians that Lincoln and the Radicals were coming closer together in early 1865 is difficult to reconcile with a comment Lincoln made to his secretary John Nicolay in January concerning Charles Sumner, the leading Senate Radical: "He hopes to succeed in beating the president so as to change the government in its original form and making it a centralized power."[54] Here I think we come close to the heart of Lincoln's quarrel with the Radicals: he simply did not share the Radical belief that the Civil War constituted a political revolution that had fundamentally changed the relationship between the states and the federal government. Just as Lincoln's conservative constitutionalism had prevented him from acting against slavery in the states until it became necessary to

save the Union, it was now preventing him from supporting federal or congressional efforts to establish political and social equality for blacks. One likes to think,
however, that Lincoln possessed a fundamental sense
of fairness which (if he had lived) would have made
him aware of the injustice of the highly discriminatory
"black codes" passed by Southern state legislatures during Presidential Reconstruction in 1865–1866. But unless he had changed his constitutional philosophy, there
would not have been much that he could have done
about it.

This interpretation is at odds with the one that sees
the Gettysburg Address as indicative of Lincoln's endorsement of a new constitutional order, committed to
equality and not merely to individual liberty.[55] There is
no mention of emancipation in the Address, and the
"new birth of freedom" to which it refers could have
meant that a Northern victory would prove to the
world that a democratic government could sustain itself
against a rebellious minority. The claim that preservation of the Union would mean that the "government of
the people, by the people, and for the people shall not
perish from the earth" repeated almost word for word
what Lincoln had said to Congress in 1861 when he
called for the preservation of "a government of the peo-

ple, by the same people."[56] Nothing in the Gettysburg Address is clearly inconsistent with the rhetoric he employed then, well before he had decided to act decisively against slavery, to define what was at stake in the war. Lincoln had believed at the beginning of the conflict that, despite the blemish of slavery in part of the nation, the United States was essentially a democratic republic and that its dissolution might prove a fatal blow to the cause of democracy throughout the world.

The hypothetical question of what Lincoln would have done and thought had he survived into the Reconstruction period is of course unanswerable. One possibility is that his policies would have been similar to those of his successor, Andrew Johnson, but would have been implemented with greater political finesse and effectiveness. At the war's end Lincoln and Johnson seemed to have similarly conservative views of what the Constitution permitted. But it is also possible, and perhaps somewhat more likely, that Lincoln's views would have evolved and moved him closer to the Radicals in the wake of the race riots and Ku Klux Klan-like atrocities that occurred in the South. Unlike Johnson, who consistently manifested a hard-core, callous racism, Lincoln's attitude toward blacks had become more favorable and sympathetic in the last years of the war, largely as a result of their military contribution to the survival of the Union. To see blacks who had served the Union being brutally mistreated by Southern whites would presumably have evoked a strong emotional reaction in Lincoln and would possibly have led to forceful intervention.

Perhaps the most incisive general evaluation of Lincoln's relationship to African Americans can be found in the "Oration in Memory of Abraham Lincoln" delivered by Frederick Douglass on the occasion of the dedication of The Freedmen's Memorial Monument to Abraham Lincoln in 1876. In the portion most often quoted, Douglass described Lincoln as "preeminently a white man's president, entirely devoted to the welfare of white men," who "was ready and willing at any time during the first years of his administration to deny, postpone, and sacrifice the rights of humanity in the colored people to promote the welfare of the white people of this country." Whereas white Americans were "the children of Abraham Lincoln," blacks were "only his stepchildren, children by adoption, children by forces of circumstance and necessity." But after so vividly describing Lincoln's limitations and shortcomings from a black perspective, Douglass went on to give him credit for leading a successful movement against slavery, even if for him the principal beneficiaries of emancipation were whites rather than blacks. Making an early contribution to the apotheosis of Lincoln that characterized black thought until the 1960s, Douglass concluded on a very positive note: "Viewed from genuine abolition ground, Mr. Lincoln seemed tardy, cold, dull, and indifferent; but measuring him by the sentiment of his country, a sentiment he was bound as a statesman to consult, he was swift, zealous, radical, and determined."[57]

NOTES

INDEX

Notes

Preface

1. George M. Fredrickson, "A Man but Not a Brother: Abraham Lincoln and Racial Equality," *Journal of Southern History*, 41 (1975), 39–58.

2. In my article I accepted, albeit with some uncertainty, the testimony of General Benjamin F. Butler that Lincoln was giving favorable consideration to Butler's scheme to send freed African Americans to Panama, where they could be employed in digging a canal. Since this alleged exchange took place late in the war, it suggested to me that Lincoln never fully abandoned his hopes of eliminating or alleviating "the race problem" by colonizing blacks outside of the United States. But

Mark E. Neely, Jr. argued effectively in 1979 that Butler's testimony was false. See his "Abraham Lincoln and Black Colonization: Benjamin Butler's Spurious Testimony," *Civil War History*, 25 (1979), 77–83.

1. A Clash of Images

1. Quoted in Allen C. Guelzo, "How Abraham Lincoln Lost the Black Vote: Lincoln and Emancipation in the African American Mind," *Journal of the Abraham Lincoln Association*, 25 (Summer 2004), 12.

2. Philip S. Foner, ed., *W. E. B. Du Bois Speaks: Speeches and Addresses, 1890–1919* (New York, 1970), 261.

3. W. E. B. Du Bois, *Writings*, The Library of America (New York, 1986), 1196.

4. Ibid., 1197–1198.

5. Including my own earlier effort: "A Man but Not a Brother: Abraham Lincoln and Racial Equality," *Journal of Southern History*, 41 (1975), 39–58.

6. On the multiplicity of Lincoln images, see Barry Schwartz, *Abraham Lincoln and the Forge of National Memory* (Chicago, 2000).

7. See ibid., 217–222.

8. Gary Wills, *Lincoln at Gettysburg: The Words That Remade America* (New York, 1992); George P. Fletcher, *Our Secret*

Constitution: How Lincoln Redefined American Democracy (New York, 2001).

9. See Willmoore Kendall, *The Conservative Affirmation* (New York, 1963), and M. E. Bradford, *Who We Are: Observations of a Southern Conservative* (Athens, Ga., 1985). See also Wills, *Lincoln at Gettysburg*, 39, 269n.

10. Merrill D. Peterson, *Lincoln in American Memory* (New York, 1994), 168–170; Schwartz, *Abraham Lincoln and the Forge of National Memory*, 217–222.

11. David Herbert Donald, *Lincoln* (New York, 1995); Richard J. Carwardine, *Lincoln* (Harlow, England, 2003).

12. See J. G. Randall, *Lincoln the President*, 3 vols. (New York, 1945–1953), and Avery Craven, *The Coming of the Civil War* (Chicago, 1957).

13. The most thorough and influential of the neo-abolitionist works of the 1960s was James M. McPherson, *The Struggle for Equality: Abolitionists and the Negro in the Civil War and Reconstruction* (Princeton, 1964). (In more recent works, McPherson has presented Lincoln in a more favorable light than in this first book.) For a range of neo-abolitionist opinion that clearly sides with the radicals against Lincoln, see also Martin Duberman, ed., *The Antislavery Vanguard* (Princeton, 1965).

14. My essay, "A Man but Not a Brother," might be taken as an example. See also Don E. Fehrenbacher, "Only His

Stepchildren: Lincoln and the Negro," in *Lincoln in Text and Context: Collected Essays* (Stanford, 1987), 95–112, which was originally published in *Civil War History* in 1974.

15. LaWanda Cox, *Lincoln and Black Freedom: A Study in Presidential Leadership* (Columbia, S.C., 1981); see especially chap. 5. See also Peyton McCrary, *Abraham Lincoln and Reconstruction: The Louisiana Experiment* (Princeton, 1978).

16. Allen C. Guelzo, *Lincoln's Emancipation Proclamation: The End of Slavery in America* (New York, 2004), 4, 25.

17. See Harry V. Jaffa, *A New Birth of Freedom: Abraham Lincoln and the Coming of the Civil War* (Lanham, Md., 2000).

18. William Lee Miller, *Lincoln's Virtues: An Ethical Biography* (New York, 2003). Quotation on p. 222.

19. Guelzo, *Lincoln's Emancipation Proclamation*, 11.

20. Richard Striner, *Father Abraham: Lincoln's Relentless Struggle to End Slavery* (New York, 2006), 59.

21. Ibid., 147.

22. Ibid., 149.

23. Quoted in Guelzo, "How Abraham Lincoln Lost the Black Vote," 11.

24. Benjamin Quarles, *Lincoln and the Negro* (New York, 1962), 249.

25. Eric Foner, review of *Forced into Glory*, *Los Angeles Times*, April 9, 2000.

26. Quoted in Guelzo, "How Abraham Lincoln Lost the Black Vote," 18.

27. Lerone Bennett, "Was Abe Lincoln a White Supremacist?", *Ebony*, February 1968, 35–38. His well-received survey of African American history, *Before the Mayflower* (Chicago, 1961), went through six editions. His *Black Power, U.S.A.: The Human Side of Reconstruction, 1867–1877* (Chicago, 1967) presented a new view of Reconstruction that emphasized black achievement in the face of adversity.

28. Lerone Bennett, *Forced into Glory: Abraham Lincoln's White Dream* (Chicago, 2000), 251.

29. On the contribution of blacks to their own emancipation, see Ira Berlin, "Who Freed the Slaves? Emancipation and Its Meaning," in David W. Blight and Brooks D. Simpson, eds., *Union and Emancipation: Essays on Politics and Race in the Civil War Era* (Kent, Ohio, 1997), 105–121.

30. Bennett, *Forced into Glory*, 618.

31. *The New York Times*, August 27, 2000.

32. Actually there's a tension, if not a contradiction, that arises when Bennett highlights Lincoln's advocacy of colonization while denying that he was in any sense antislavery. The evidence suggests that Lincoln saw colonization as part of a gradual emancipation process rather than as an alternative to it. But we'll come back to this issue later.

33. Bennett, *Forced into Glory*, 626.

34. Michael Lind, *What Lincoln Believed: The Values and Convictions of America's Greatest President* (New York, 2004), 15.

35. Guelzo, *Emancipation Proclamation*, 247–248.

36. Lind, *What Lincoln Believed*, 292.

37. Ibid., 224–225.

38. Ibid., 206–208.

39. Schwartz, *Abraham Lincoln and the Forge of National Memory*, 2, 4.

40. Jaffa, *New Birth of Freedom*, passim.

41. See David Brion Davis, *Inhuman Bondage: The Rise and Fall of Slavery in the New World* (New York, 2006), 141–156, and Gary B. Nash, *The Forgotten Fifth: African Americans in the Age of Revolution* (Cambridge, Mass., 2006).

42. See Davis, *Inhuman Bondage*, 175–204, and Nash, *Forgotten Fifth*, 123–168.

43. See Davis, *Inhuman Bondage*, 268–296, for a concise account of these developments. The best detailed account is still David M. Potter, *Impending Crisis, 1848–1861*, completed and edited by Don E. Fehrenbacher (New York, 1976).

44. See Potter, *Impending Crisis*.

45. Leon F. Litwack, *North of Slavery: The Negro in the Free States* (Chicago, 1961); Eugene H. Berwanger, *The Frontier Against Slavery: Western Anti-Negro Prejudice and the*

Slavery Extension Controversy (Urbana, Ill., 1967); Charles N. Zucker, "The Free Negro Question: Race Relations in Ante-Bellum Illinois," doctoral dissertation, Northwestern University, 1972.

46. Berwanger, *Frontier Against Slavery*, 22–29. A fuller account of these developments can be found in Zucker, "The Free Negro Question," 27–84.

47. Zucker, "The Free Negro Question," 40–43, 157–169.

48. Quoted in Berwanger, *Frontier Against Slavery*, 31.

49. Zucker, "The Free Negro Question," 311–312.

50. Berwanger, *Frontier Against Slavery*, 29–31. Quotation on p. 29. See also Zucker, "The Free Negro Question," 313–314.

51. Don E. Fehrenbacher, *Prelude to Greatness: Lincoln in the 1850s* (Stanford, 1962).

2. Free Soil, Free Labor, and Free White Men

1. Abraham Lincoln, *Speeches and Writings, 1832–1858*, ed. Don E. Fehrenbacher, The Library of America (New York, 1989), 471. This is the first of two volumes; the second covers the years 1859–1865. Further references to these volumes will be abbreviated as *S&W*, vol. 1 or 2. I have chosen to rely mainly on the Library of America *Speeches and Writings* rather than on the more commonly used *Collected Works of Abraham Lincoln* in 9 volumes, ed-

ited by Roy P. Basler (New Brunswick, N.J., 1955). All of the essential speeches and writings, authoritatively edited by Fehrenbacher, can be found in *S&W,* and some utterances that have subsequently proved to be questionable or spurious have been eliminated. On a few occasions I have resorted to the *Collected Works* for material that helped me to make a point even though its general significance was not sufficient to merit its inclusion in *S&W.*

2. Douglas L. Wilson, *Honor's Voice: The Transformation of Abraham Lincoln* (New York, 1998), 164–166.

3. *S&W,* vol. 1, 18.

4. Ibid., 227–229.

5. *S&W,* vol. 2, 161.

6. On religion and slavery in Lincoln's childhood, see Michael Burlingame, *The Inner World of Abraham Lincoln* (Urbana, Ill., 1994), 22, and Allen C. Guelzo, *Abraham Lincoln: Redeemer President* (Grand Rapids, Mich., 1999), 36–38.

7. Burlingame, *Inner World,* 37.

8. *S&W,* vol. 2, 259.

9. Ibid., 144. For an excellent description and analysis of this free-labor ideology, see Eric Foner, *Free Soil, Free Labor, Free Men: The Ideology of the Republican Party Before the Civil War* (New York, 1970).

10. *S&W,* vol. 1, 112.

11. Ibid., 90.

12. David Freeman Hawke, ed., *Herndon's Lincoln: The True Story of a Great Life* (Indianapolis, 1970), 153.

13. *S&W,* vol. 1, 382.

14. Ibid., 29.

15. Ibid., 33.

16. Ibid., 32; see also George M. Fredrickson, "The Search for Order and Community," in Cullom Davis et al., eds., *The Public and Private Lincoln: Contemporary Perspectives* (Carbondale, Ill., 1979), 86–98.

17. This is the argument of my essay, "The Search for Order and Community."

18. *S&W,* vol. 1, 333.

19. See George M. Fredrickson, *The Black Image in the White Mind: The Debate on Afro-American Character and Destiny, 1817–1914* (New York, 1971), chap. 1.

20. Barry Schwartz, *Lincoln and the Forge of National Memory* (Chicago, 2000), 3.

21. Roy P. Basler, ed., *The Collected Works of Abraham Lincoln* (New Brunswick, N.J., 1953), vol. 1, 210.

22. Charles N. Zucker, "The Free Negro Question: Race Relations in Ante-bellum Illinois," doctoral dissertation, Northwestern University, 1972, 182–183.

23. *S&W,* vol. 1, 520.

24. Don E. Fehrenbacher and Virginia Fehrenbacher, eds., *Recollected Words of Abraham Lincoln* (Stanford, 1996), 384.

25. *S&W*, vol. 1, 269.

26. Lerone Bennett, *Forced into Glory: Abraham Lincoln's White Dream* (Chicago, 2000), 83, 222, 303.

27. A recent book that stresses the racial egalitarianism of the abolitionists is Paul Goodman, *Of One Blood: Abolitionists and the Origins of Racial Equality* (Berkeley, 1998).

28. *S&W*, vol. 1, 271.

29. Although in fact popular sovereignty had found its way into the Compromise of 1850 as a device for determining the future of slavery in the New Mexico territory.

30. *S&W*, vol. 1, 447.

31. Ibid., 315.

32. Ibid., 316.

33. Ibid., 85.

34. Ibid., 331.

35. This view was put forth most emphatically by Richard Striner in *Father Abraham* (2006), a book which is described in some detail in Chapter 1.

36. *S&W*, vol. 1, 328–329.

37. Ibid., 397–398.

38. Ibid., 398.

39. Ibid., 401.

40. Ibid., 360.

41. Ibid., 417.

42. Ibid., 426.

43. Douglas L. Wilson and Rodney O. Davis, eds., *Herndon's Informants: Letters, Interviews, and Statements about Abraham Lincoln* (Urbana, Ill., 1998), 163.

44. *S&W*, vol. 2, 17.

45. Ibid., 193.

46. *S&W*, vol. 1, 426.

47. *S&W*, vol. 2, 35.

48. See Don E. Fehrenbacher, *Prelude to Greatness: Lincoln in the 1850s* (Stanford, 1962).

49. *S&W*, vol. 1, 504–505.

50. Ibid., 512.

51. *S&W*, vol. 2, 259.

52. *S&W*, vol. 1, 637.

53. It is true, however, that Lincoln did make one statement in 1858 that sounded like a repudiation of racial discrimination. In a speech in Chicago before the debates, he called upon his audience to "discard all this quibbling about this man and the other man—this race and that race and the other race being inferior and therefore they must be placed in an inferior position . . . Let us unite as one people throughout this land until we shall once more stand up declaring that all men are created equal" (ibid., 458). In none of his other prewar speeches did Lincoln express sentiments of this kind. There may in

fact be an element of hypocrisy here; but it seems more likely that Lincoln was pandering to the quasi-abolitionists who would be part of an audience in Chicago than that he was pretending to be a white supremacist in the rest of the state.

54. *S&W*, vol. 1, 636.

55. Ibid., 514–515.

56. Ibid., 808.

57. Harmannus Hoetink, *The Two Variants of Caribbean Race Relations: A Contribution to the Sociology of Segmented Societies* (London, 1967), 106–110 and passim.

58. *S&W*, vol. 1, 717.

59. Ibid., 360–361.

60. Ibid., 740.

61. See Fehrenbacher, *Prelude to Greatness*.

62. *S&W*, vol. 2, 57, 68.

63. Ibid., 112–119. See also Harold Holzer, *Lincoln at Cooper Union: The Speech That Made Abraham Lincoln President* (New York, 2004), 126–128 and passim.

64. *S&W*, vol. 2, 120; italics in the original.

65. There are several recollections to this effect in Wilson and Davis, eds., *Herndon's Informants*. See, for example, pp. 183–184, 429, 457, 494.

66. Foner, *Free Soil, Free Labor, Free Men*, 286.

67. On racism as conformity, see Thomas F. Pettigrew, *Racially Separate or Together* (New York, 1969).

3. Becoming an Emancipator

1. David Potter, *The South and the Sectional Conflict* (Baton Rouge, 1968), 157.

2. Abraham Lincoln, *Speeches and Writings, 1859–1865*, The Library of America (New York, 1989), 585–586. There are two volumes in this series; the first covers the years 1832–1858. Further references to these volumes will be abbreviated as *S&W*, vol. 1 or 2.

3. *S&W*, vol. 2, 213.

4. Roy P. Basler, ed., *The Collected Works of Abraham Lincoln* (New Brunswick, N.J., 1953), vol. 4, 169.

5. *S&W*, vol. 2, 222.

6. Ibid., 250.

7. Ibid., 259.

8. Don E. Fehrenbacher and Virginia Fehrenbacher, eds., *Recollected Words of Abraham Lincoln* (Stanford, 1996), 455–456.

9. Ibid., 164. The Fehrenbachers are not completely confident of the accuracy of Jesse Frémont's recollection of what Lincoln said. But it is not inconsistent with other reported utterances of 1861.

10. *S&W*, vol. 2, 318–319.

11. Ibid., 269.

12. Ibid., 292.

13. Ibid., 291–292.

14. Ibid., 355.

15. Fehrenbacher and Fehrenbacher, eds., *Recollected Words*, 62.

16. *S&W*, vol. 2, 319.

17. Fehrenbacher and Fehrenbacher, eds., *Recollected Words*, 64.

18. *S&W*, vol. 2, 276–278. See also Allen C. Guelzo, *Lincoln's Emancipation Proclamation: The End of Slavery in America* (New York, 2004), 57, 94–95.

19. *S&W*, vol. 2, 307–308.

20. Basler, ed., *Collected Works of Abraham Lincoln*, vol. 5, 146 (notes 1 and 7).

21. William C. Harris, *With Charity for All: Lincoln and the Restoration of the Union* (Lexington, Ky., 1997), 36–39.

22. George M. Fredrickson, *The Inner Civil War: Northern Intellectuals and the Crisis of the Union* (New York, 1965), 113–115.

23. The text of the first draft can be found in Guelzo, *Lincoln's Emancipation Proclamation*, 253–254.

24. *S&W*, vol. 2, 358.

25. Ibid., 368. "This continent" referred to the Americas generally, not just the United States or North America.

26. Ibid., 365.

27. Ira Berlin, "Who Freed the Slaves? Emancipation and Its Meaning," in David W. Blight and Brooks D.

Simpson, eds., *Union and Emancipation: Essays on Politics and Race in the Civil War Era* (Kent, Ohio, 1997), 112.

28. Guelzo, *Lincoln's Emancipation Proclamation*, 212–213.

29. *S&W*, vol. 2, 353–355; italics added.

30. Ibid., 355.

31. This account is based mainly on Benjamin Quarles, *Lincoln and the Negro* (New York, 1962), 108–114 and 191–194.

32. *The Diary of Gideon Welles* (Boston, 1911), 152.

33. *S&W*, vol. 2, 406–407.

34. Ibid., 412–413.

35. Ibid., 413. Michael Lind is an exception; see *What Lincoln Believed*, 205, which is discussed in Chapter 1.

36. This is the argument of Don E. Fehrenbacher in "Only His Stepchildren: Lincoln and the Negro," in *Lincoln in Text and Context* (Stanford, 1987), 95–112, and of Michael Vorenberg in "Abraham Lincoln and the Politics of Black Colonization," *Journal of the Abraham Lincoln Association*, 14 (Summer 1993), 22–45.

37. Phillip Shaw Paludan ably presents the case for Lincoln's sincerity in "Lincoln and Colonization: Policy or Propaganda," *Journal of the Abraham Lincoln Association*, 25 (Summer 2004), 23–37.

38. See William C. Harris, "The Hampton Roads Conference: A Final Test of Lincoln's Political Leadership,"

Journal of the Abraham Lincoln Association, 21 (Winter 2000), 31–61, and William E. Gienapp, *Abraham Lincoln and Civil War America: A Biography* (New York, 2002), 182.

39. Tyler Dennett, ed., *Lincoln and the Civil War in the Diaries and Letters of John Hay* (New York, 1939), 203.

40. See George M. Fredrickson, *The Black Image in the White Mind: The Debate on Afro-American Character and Destiny, 1817–1914* (New York, 1971), 166–168.

41. Fehrenbacher and Fehrenbacher, eds., *Recollected Words*, 199.

42. *S&W*, vol. 2, 365.

43. Ibid., 490.

44. Ibid., 497–499.

45. Fehrenbacher and Fehrenbacher, eds., *Recollected Words*, 144.

46. Ibid., 579.

47. Ibid., 699.

48. *S&W*, vol. 1, 637. See also Don E. Fehrenbacher, "Lincoln and the Constitution," in Cullom Davis et al., eds., *The Public and Private Lincoln: Contemporary Perspectives* (Carbondale, Ill., 1979), 121–136.

49. See William C. Harris, *Lincoln's Last Months* (Cambridge, Mass., 2004), 214; Harris, *With Charity for All*, 125–126; and Fehrenbacher in *Public and Private Lincoln*, 124.

50. Harris, *With Charity for All*, 186–190; *S&W*, vol. 2, 605–606.

51. Fehrenbacher and Fehrenbacher, eds., *Recollected Words*, 229.

52. Dennett, ed., *Diaries and Letters of John Hay*, 244–245.

53. Fehrenbacher and Fehrenbacher, eds., *Recollected Words*, 291.

54. Ibid., 349.

55. See especially Gary Wills, *Lincoln at Gettysburg: The Words That Changed America* (New York, 1992), and George P. Fletcher, *The Secret Constitution: How Lincoln Redefined American Democracy* (New York, 2001). As we have seen, Don E. Fehrenbacher and William C. Harris argue the contrary, as do I.

56. *S&W*, vol. 2, 250.

57. Philip S. Foner, ed., *The Life and Writings of Frederick Douglass*, vol. 4 (New York, 1955), 312, 314, 316.

Index

Index